Pressure Cooker Curry Magic: 98 Quick and Flavorful Recipes for Authentic Curries

The Curry Corner

Copyright © 2023 The Curry Corner
All rights reserved.

Contents

- INTRODUCTION 7
- 1. Chicken Tikka Masala 9
- 2. Vegetable Korma 10
- 3. Lamb Rogan Josh 11
- 4. Chana Masala 12
- 5. Palak Paneer 13
- 6. Butter Chicken 14
- 7. Egg Curry 15
- 8. Aloo Gobi 16
- 9. Beef Vindaloo 18
- 10. Dal Makhani 19
- 11. Fish Curry 20
- 12. Mushroom Masala 21
- 13. Paneer Tikka Masala 22
- 14. Chicken Biryani 23
- 15. Baingan Bharta 24
- 16. Goat Curry 25
- 17. Rajma Masala 26
- 18. Vegetable Pulao 28
- 19. Chicken Korma 29
- 20. Malai Kofta 30
- 21. Prawn Curry 31
- 22. Aloo Palak 32
- 23. Pork Vindaloo 33
- 24. Masoor Dal 34
- 25. Fish Biryani 35
- 26. Mushroom Matar 36
- 27. Mutton Curry 37

28. Black-eyed Pea Curry ... 38
29. Jeera Rice ... 39
30. Chicken Curry ... 40
31. Mixed Vegetable Curry ... 41
32. Chicken Jalfrezi ... 42
33. Vegetable Biryani ... 44
34. Shahi Paneer ... 45
35. Shrimp Curry ... 46
36. Aloo Matar ... 47
37. Lamb Korma ... 48
38. Dal Tadka ... 49
39. Fish Korma ... 50
40. Baingan Mirch Ka Salan ... 51
41. Keema Matar ... 52
42. Chole Bhature ... 53
43. Chicken Vindaloo ... 55
44. Paneer Butter Masala ... 56
45. Goat Biryani ... 57
46. Bhindi Masala ... 58
47. Pork Curry ... 59
48. Masoor Pulao ... 60
49. Egg Biryani ... 61
50. Mushroom Curry ... 62
51. Mutton Korma ... 63
52. Navratan Korma ... 64
53. Prawn Biryani ... 65
54. Aloo Baingan ... 66
55. Chicken Saagwala ... 67
56. Rajma Pulao ... 69

57. Chicken Pulao 70
58. Paneer Bhurji 71
59. Fish Tikka Masala 72
60. Baingan Patiala 73
61. Beef Curry 74
62. Dal Fry 75
63. Vegetable Khichdi 76
64. Chicken Dhansak 77
65. Matar Paneer 78
66. Goat Pulao 80
67. Lauki Chana Dal 81
68. Shrimp Biryani 82
69. Aloo Methi 83
70. Lamb Curry 84
71. Kala Chana Curry 85
72. Chicken Madras 86
73. Capsicum Masala 86
74. Masoor Khichdi 88
75. Fish Fry 89
76. Mushroom Pulao 89
77. Chicken Handi 91
78. Palak Corn 92
79. Baingan Bhurta 92
80. Keema Pulao 93
81. Rajma Chawal 95
82. Chicken Sukka 96
83. Paneer Jalfrezi 97
84. Prawn Masala 98
85. Aloo Dum 99

86. Lamb Biryani 100
87. Vegetable Sambar 101
88. Chicken Chettinad 102
89. Methi Matar Malai 103
90. Mushroom Rice 104
91. Mutton Biryani 105
92. Chole Pulao 106
93. Egg Fried Rice 107
94. Aloo Gajar 108
95. Masoor Curry 109
96. Vegetable Curry 110
97. Chicken Kadai 111
98. Paneer Tikki Masala 112
CONCLUSION 114

INTRODUCTION

Pressure Cooker Curry Magic: 98 Quick and Flavorful Recipes for Authentic Curries

Welcome to Pressure Cooker Curry Magic! Through this cookbook, you will discover the delicious flavors of authentic curries and the wonders of pressure cooking. From Indian-style to Southeast Asian-inspired dishes, you'll find all of your favorite curry dishes easy to make and full of flavor.

With pressure cooking, you'll be able to quickly and easily make 98 different curry recipes. Our recipes combine fragrant spices, fresh herbs, and other flavorful ingredients that come together in harmony to give you a meal you and your family will love. Pressure cooking also brings out the best in your ingredients, keeping the food moist and flavorful despite the quick cooking time.

From creamy korma to hearty makhani, to spicy vindaloo and everything in between, you'll find recipes for all your favorite curries, plus plenty of new and delicious selections. Our recipes make use of grated coconut, coconut milk, ground spices, curry paste, and more—all of which come together to make these recipes truly magical and authentic.

Moreover, while the pressure cooker makes the process faster, you'll still find that the recipes in Pressure Cooker Curry Magic incorporate many traditional Indian and Southeast Asian techniques and ingredients. For instance, you'll learn how to make your own garam masala and biryani, plus you'll find recipes for unique dishes like tamarind lentils and eggplant chutney.

Each dish offers its own tantalizing flavor, so you'll never be bored. From starters and appetizers, to main dishes and side dishes, you'll discover a world of delicious curries just waiting to be cooked. And because of the pressure cooker, the recipes are fast and easy, so you can spend more time enjoying your meal.

So dive into Pressure Cooker Curry Magic today and see how easy it is to cook up a wonderful curry dinner that will please every palate! With 98 quick, flavorful recipes for authentic curries, you're guaranteed to have a delicious meal every time.

1. Chicken Tikka Masala

Chicken Tikka Masala is a fragrant, rich and creamy Indian curry bursting with flavor.
Serving: 6
Preparation Time: 15 minutes
Ready Time: 45 minutes

Ingredients:
- 2 lb boneless, skinless chicken thighs, cut into 1" cubes
- 2 onions, diced
- 1/3 cup fresh ginger, grated
- 4 cloves garlic, finely minced
- 2 tablespoons garam masala
- 1 tablespoon curry powder
- 1 teaspoon ground cumin
- 1 teaspoon ground coriander
- 2 tablespoons tomato paste
- 2 tablespoons olive oil
- 2 tablespoons plain yogurt
- 1 teaspoon salt
- 1 teaspoon sugar
- 1 cup full-fat canned coconut milk
- 2 tablespoons fresh cilantro, finely chopped

Instructions:
1. Preheat oven to 375°F (190°C).
2. In a medium bowl, combine chicken cubes with 1 tablespoon of garam masala and 1 teaspoon of salt.
3. Spread chicken cubes out onto a baking sheet lined with parchment paper and bake in preheated oven for 25 minutes, stirring halfway through.
4. Meanwhile, heat olive oil in a large skillet over medium heat. Add in onions and cook until softened.
5. Add ginger, garlic, curry powder, cumin, coriander, and remaining garam masala. Cook until fragrant, about 30 seconds.
6. Stir in tomato paste and yogurt. Simmer for 2 minutes.
7. Add chicken cubes with juices from baking sheet and stir to combine.

8. Slowly stir in coconut milk, sugar, and fresh cilantro. Simmer for 15 minutes.
9. Serve over cooked basmati rice and garnish with additional cilantro, if desired. Enjoy!

Nutrition information:
Per serving: 420 calories; 22.8 g fat; 32.6 g carbohydrates; 20.7 g protein; 4.5 g fiber; 948 mg sodium.

2. Vegetable Korma

Vegetable Korma is a delicious Indian dish with an array of vegetables simmered in a creamy tomato-coconut based sauce.
Serving: 4
Preparation time: 15 minutes
Ready time: 45 minutes

Ingredients:
- 4 tablespoons vegetable oil
- 2 onions, thinly sliced
- 5 cloves garlic, minced
- 2 tablespoons minced fresh ginger
- 2 teaspoons ground cumin
- 1 teaspoon garam masala
- 1 teaspoon ground coriander
- 1 teaspoon ground turmeric
- ¼ teaspoon cayenne pepper
- 2 large tomatoes, chopped
- 2 tablespoons tomato paste
- 2 tablespoons honey
- 2 cups vegetable stock
- 1 (13.5-ounce) can coconut milk
- 1 bay leaf
- 3 cups mixed vegetables, such as cauliflower, carrots, peas, and bell peppers
- Salt and freshly ground black pepper
- ½ cup chopped cilantro

Instructions:
1. Heat vegetable oil in a large saucepan over medium heat. Add onions and garlic, and cook, stirring often, until onions are golden brown, about 10 minutes.
2. Add ginger, cumin, garam masala, coriander, turmeric, and cayenne pepper; stir to combine.
3. Add tomatoes, tomato paste, honey, vegetable stock, coconut milk, and bay leaf; bring to a rolling boil. Reduce heat to low and simmer for 20 minutes.
4. Add vegetables and cook, stirring occasionally, until vegetables are tender, about 10 minutes.
5. Season with salt and pepper to taste, then stir in cilantro.

Nutrition information: Per serving: 294 calories, 22 grams fat, 8 grams protein, 18 grams carbohydrate, 4 grams fiber, 804 milligrams sodium.

3. Lamb Rogan Josh

Lamb Rogan Josh is a traditional Kashmiri Indian dish made with boneless cubes of lamb, sautéed onions, and a mixture of spices cooked in a tomato-based sauce. This long-simmered, flavorful dish is perfect for special occasions.
Serving: Serves 4
Preparation time: 15 minutes
Ready time: 1 hour

Ingredients:
- 2 tablespoons vegetable oil
- 1 pound of boneless lamb cubes
- 1 large onion, finely diced
- 1-2 teaspoons minced garlic
- 2 teaspoons ground turmeric
- 2 teaspoon ground cumin
- 2 teaspoon ground coriander
- 2 teaspoons ground cardamom
- 2 teaspoons paprika
- 1/4 teaspoon cayenne

- 2 ripe tomatoes, diced
- 2 cups of water
- Salt and pepper, to taste

Instructions:
1. Heat the oil in a large skillet over medium-high heat.
2. Add the onions and stir-fry until lightly browned.
3. Add the garlic, spices, and lamb cubes to the onions and cook until the lamb is browned.
4. Add the tomato and stir-fry for another 2 minutes.
5. Pour in the water and bring to a boil.
6. Lower the heat, cover the pot, and simmer the dish for 30 minutes, or until the lamb is cooked through.
7. Season the dish with salt and pepper, to taste.

Nutrition information:
Calories: 350
Total fat: 17 g
Cholesterol: 65 mg
Sodium: 500 mg
Carbohydrates: 14 g
Protein: 30 g

4. Chana Masala

Chana Masala is an Indian curry dish made with chickpeas, tomatoes, and traditional spices. It is a great vegan dish that is both flavorful and hearty.
Serving: 4
Preparation Time: 25 minutes
Ready Time: 55 minutes

Ingredients:
- 2 tablespoons canola oil
- 1 teaspoon mustard seeds
- 1 onion, chopped
- 2 cloves garlic, minced
- 1 teaspoon ground cumin

- 1 teaspoon ground coriander
- 1 teaspoon garam masala
- 1 can (14.5 ounces) diced tomatoes
- 1 can (14.5 ounces) chickpeas, drained
- Salt and pepper to taste

Instructions:
1. Heat oil in a large skillet over medium heat.
2. Add mustard seeds and cook until they start to pop, about 30 seconds.
3. Add onion and garlic and cook until soft, about 3 minutes.
4. Add cumin, coriander, and garam masala and cook until fragrant, about 1 minute.
5. Stir in the tomatoes and their juices and bring to a simmer.
6. Add the chickpeas and season with salt and pepper.
7. Simmer for 15 minutes.
8. Serve over rice or with naan.

Nutrition information: per serving: 280 calories, 10 g fat, 5 g saturated fat, 36 g carbohydrate, 10 g fiber, 6 g protein

5. Palak Paneer

Palak Paneer is an Indian curry dish made primarily from pureed spinach and paneer (Indian cheese) cooked in a tongue-tingling combination of spices.
Serving: 4
Preparation Time: 15 minutes
Ready Time: 25 minutes

Ingredients:
- 5 cups of fresh spinach, washed and finely chopped
- 1 block of Paneer, cubed about 1/4 inch
- 2-3 tablespoons of oil
- 1 teaspoon of cumin
- 1 teaspoon of garam masala
- 1 teaspoon of ground coriander
- 1 teaspoon of red chili powder
- 1 teaspoon of turmeric powder

- 1 teaspoon of mustard seeds
- 4-5 cloves of garlic, crushed
- 1 finely chopped onion
- 2 tablespoons of fresh cream
- Salt to taste

Instructions:
1. Heat the oil in a large pan and add the cumin seeds, mustard seeds and garlic.
2. Once they start to sizzle, add the chopped onion and cook until translucent.
3. Then add the chopped spinach and cook for 5 minutes.
4. Add the garam masala, coriander powder, red chili powder and turmeric powder and mix well.
5. Add the cubed paneer and cook for 5 minutes.
6. Add the fresh cream, salt to taste and cook for about 5 minutes.
7. Serve the Palak Paneer with steamed rice or naan.

Nutrition information:
Calories: 350 kcal, Total Fat: 24 g, Saturated Fat: 12 g, Trans Fat: 0 g, Cholesterol: 72 mg, Sodium: 300 mg, Total Carbohydrate: 15 g, Dietary Fiber: 6 g, Sugars: 4 g, Protein: 19 g.

6. Butter Chicken

Butter chicken is a popular North Indian recipe of tender, succulent chicken in a creamy and spiced tomato gravy.
Serving: 4
Preparation time: 20 min
Ready time: 50 min

Ingredients:
- 500g chicken leg cubes
- 1 tablespoon ginger and garlic paste
- 2 tablespoons oil
- 1 teaspoon cumin seeds
- 1 teaspoon coriander powder
- 1 teaspoon red chilli powder

- 1 teaspoon garam masala powder
- 2 tablespoons butter
- 2 green chillies, chopped
- 180g plain yoghurt, lightlypounded
- 300ml tomato puree
- 150g butter, melted
- 1 teaspoon sugar
- Salt, to taste

Instructions:
1. Heat the oil in a deep pan.
2. Add the cumin seeds, ginger and garlic paste, corianderpowder, red chilli pepper and garam masalapowder, and stir-fry for few seconds.
3. Add the chicken cubes and fry for few minutes on a medium heat. Turn offthe heat.
4. Add the yoghurt, tomato puree, butter, green chillies, sugar andsalt, and mix everything together.
5. Simmer for 25 minutes on a low heat, or until the chicken iscooked.
6. Finally add the melted butter and mix everything together.
7. Serve the butter chicken with hot chapatis or naan breads.

Nutrition information:
Each serving of butter chicken contains approximately 300 calories, 26g of fat, 21g of protein, and 10g of carbohydrates.

7. Egg Curry

Deliciously spiced, Egg Curry is an egg-based Indian dish that is full of flavor. With a creamy tomato-based sauce and a complex medley of spices, this curry will be sure to tantalize your taste buds for an authentic Indian culinary experience.
Serving: 4-6
Preparation Time: 15 minutes
Ready Time: 45 minutes

Ingredients:
- 5-6 Eggs
- 1 Onion, finely chopped

- 2 Tomatoes, finely chopped
- 2 tablespoons Ginger-Garlic Paste
- 1 teaspoon Turmeric Powder
- 2 tablespoons Coriander Powder
- 2 tablespoons Cardamom Powder
- 2 tablespoons Cumin Powder
- 2 tablespoons Red Chili Powder
- 1 teaspoon Garam Masala
- Salt to taste
- 2 tablespoons Vegetable Oil

Instructions:
1. Boil eggs and peel them.
2. Heat oil in a pan.
3. Add onions and sauté until golden brown.
4. Add ginger-garlic paste and sauté for a few minutes.
5. Add chopped tomatoes and all the spice powders.
6. Sauté for 2 minutes and then add a cup of water.
7. Cook for 5-7 minutes until the mixture thickens.
8. Add the boiled eggs and mix gently.
9. Cook the egg curry for at least 12-15 minutes.
10. Add garam masala and salt to taste.
11. Serve the egg curry.

Nutrition information:
Calories: 124
Total Fat: 10g
Cholesterol: 187mg
Total Carbohydrates: 7g
Protein: 6g
Sodium: 228mg

8. Aloo Gobi

Aloo Gobi is a traditional Punjabi dish made by cooking potatoes and cauliflower in a spicy onion-tomato gravy. It is a vegan and vegetarian delight, and a popular dish for many in India and across the world.
Serving: Serves 4

Preparation time: 10 minutes
Ready time: 35 minutes

Ingredients:
- 3 tablespoons oil
- 1 tablespoon cumin seeds
- 1 large onion, finely chopped
- 2 green chillies, finely chopped
- 2 tablespoons ginger-garlic paste
- 1 teaspoon ground turmeric
- 4-5 tomatoes, finely chopped
- 2 large potatoes, peeled and cubed
- 1 small head cauliflower, florets separated
- 1 teaspoon red chilli powder
- Salt to taste
- 1 teaspoon garam masala
- 2 tablespoons coriander leaves, finely chopped

Instructions:
1. Heat oil in a pan over medium heat. Add cumin seeds and chopped onion. Sauté until the onion is softened and lightly browned.
2. Add ginger-garlic paste and green chillies. Sauté for a few more minutes.
3. Now add ground turmeric, chopped tomatoes, cubed potatoes, and cauliflower florets. Mix everything together and cook on medium-low heat for 5 minutes.
4. Add red chilli powder, salt, and garam masala. Mix everything together and continue to cook for a further 5 minutes.
5. Add about ½ cup of water and cover the pan. Lower the heat and simmer for 20 minutes or until the vegetables are cooked through.
6. Add the coriander leaves and mix. Taste and adjust the seasoning as per taste.
7. Serve warm with chapatis, parathas, or steamed basmati rice.

Nutrition information: Per serving - Calories: 150, Total Fat: 7 g, Saturated Fat: 1 g, Trans Fat: 0 g, Cholesterol: 0 mg, Sodium: 358 mg, Carbohydrates: 19 g, Fiber: 5 g, Protein: 5 g.

9. Beef Vindaloo

Beef Vindaloo is a traditional Indian curry with a flavorful blend of spices. This delicious dish is sure to be enjoyed by the whole family.
Serving: 4
Preparation Time: 20 minutes
Ready Time: 45 minutes

Ingredients:
- 2 tablespoons cooking oil
- 2 lbs. beef chuck, diced
- 1 onion, diced
- 5 cloves garlic, minced
- 1 teaspoon fresh ginger, grated
- 2 tablespoons ground coriander
- 1 teaspoon ground cumin
- 1 teaspoon ground cayenne
- 2 tablespoons apple cider vinegar
- 2 tablespoons tomato paste
- 2 teaspoons ground cardamom
- 1 teaspoon turmeric powder
- 2 1/2 cups beef stock
- 1 teaspoon sugar
- 1/4 cup fresh cilantro, chopped

Instructions:
1. Heat oil in a large skillet or Dutch over medium-high heat.
2. Add the beef and brown on all sides, about 5 minutes.
3. Add the onion, garlic, ginger, coriander, cumin, cayenne, and vinegar. Cook until the onion is softened, about 3 minutes.
4. Stir in the tomato paste, cardamom, turmeric, and beef stock. Bring the mixture to a boil.
5. Reduce the heat and simmer, covered, until the beef is tender, about 40 minutes.
6. Uncover and stir in the sugar and cilantro. Simmer for an additional 5 minutes.
7. Serve warm with steamed rice or naan.

Nutrition information: Per Serving: 302 calories; 12.3g total fat; 49.2g protein; 5.3g carbohydrates; 0.8g fiber; 86mg cholesterol.

10. Dal Makhani

Dal Makhani is a popular Punjabi dish consisting of whole black lentils simmered overnight in a creamy, tomato-based sauce. It is savory, creamy, and subtly spiced.
Serving: 4-5
Preparation Time: 15 minutes
Ready Time: 8-9 hours

Ingredients:
- 2 cups whole black lentils (urad dal)
- 2 cans diced tomatoes
- 2 cloves garlic, minced
- 2 inches fresh ginger, minced
- 1 tablespoon garlic paste
- 2 tablespoons ghee
- 1 teaspoon garam masala
- 2 tablespoons Kashmiri red chili powder
- Salt to taste

Instructions:
1. Soak lentils overnight in a large bowl of water.
2. Drain the lentils and rinse them with cold water. Set aside.
3. Heat the ghee in a large pot over medium heat.
4. Add the garlic and ginger and sauté for a few minutes until fragrant.
5. Add the tomatoes and simmer for 8-10 minutes until the tomatoes are cooked down.
6. Add the lentils and stir to combine.
7. Add the Garam masala, chili powder, salt, and garlic paste and mix.
8. Add 4 cups of water, cover, and bring to a boil.
9. Reduce the heat to low and let simmer for 8-9 hours until the lentils are completely cooked and the sauce has thickened.
10. Serve hot with basmati rice and cream for garnish.

Nutrition information:
Per Serving:
Calories: 350

Fat: 8.5g
Carbohydrates: 62g
Protein: 16g
Saturated Fat: 5g
Sodium: 625mg
Fiber: 14g

11. Fish Curry

Fish Curry is an aromatic and flavoursome dish that is popular in many regions around the world. This particular recipe for Fish Curry takes inspiration from Indian cuisine and is best served with plain white rice or naan bread.
Serving: 4
Preparation time: 10 minutes
Ready time: 45 minutes

Ingredients:
- 500g (1 lb) of firm white fish fillets, cubed
- 1 onion, diced
- 2 cloves of garlic, minced
- 2 tablespoons of grated ginger
- 2 tablespoons of tomato paste
- 1 teaspoon of ground coriander
- 1 teaspoon of ground cumin
- 1 teaspoon of turmeric
- ¼ teaspoon of cayenne pepper
- 1 cup of coconut milk
- Salt and pepper, to taste

Instructions:
1. Heat a medium-sized saucepan over medium-high heat. Add the diced onion and sauté for about 3 minutes, until they become softened.
2. Add the garlic, ginger, and tomato paste and cook for an additional minute.
3. Add the ground coriander, cumin, and turmeric, and cook for another minute.

4. Pour in the coconut milk and stir to combine. Bring the curry to a gentle simmer, and season with salt and pepper, to taste.
5. Add the fish cubes to the saucepan and cover with a lid. Reduce the heat to low and simmer for about 25 minutes, stirring occasionally.
6. Once the fish is cooked, the curry is ready to serve.

Nutrition information: Per serving: 240 calories, 17g fat, 12g protein, 10g carbohydrate, 1g dietary fiber, 0mg cholesterol, 103mg sodium

12. Mushroom Masala

Mushroom Masala is an Indian dish packed with delicious and aromatic flavors. It's a tasty vegetarian main course that is perfect for dinner parties or everyday meals.
Serving: 6-8
Preparation Time: 15 minutes
Ready Time: 30 minutes

Ingredients:
- 2 tablespoons vegetable oil
- 1/2 teaspoon cumin seeds
- 1 cup white onions, diced
- 4-5 cloves garlic, minced
- 2 centimeters ginger, grated
- 1/2 tablespoon garam masala
- 1 tablespoon coriander powder
- 1/4 teaspoon chili powder
- 1 (14 ounce) can diced tomatoes
- 1 teaspoon sugar
- 1 pound white mushrooms, sliced
- Salt to taste
- 2-3 tablespoons fresh cilantro, minced

Instructions:
1. Heat oil in a large skillet over medium-high heat.
2. Add cumin seeds and stir for 30 seconds.

3. Add the onion, garlic, and ginger and sauté for 5 minutes until the onions are softened.
4. Add garam masala, coriander powder, and chili powder to the skillet. Sauté for 30 seconds.
5. Add the diced tomatoes and sugar to the skillet and cook for 5 minutes.
6. Add mushrooms and season with salt. Cover and cook for 8-10 minutes, or until the mushrooms are cooked through.
7. Stir in the fresh cilantro and cook for 1 minute.
8. Serve hot.

Nutrition information:
- Calories: 142 kcal
- Fat: 6.9 g
- Carbohydrate: 15.7 g
- Protein: 5.2 g
- Fiber: 2.6 g
- Sodium: 200 mg

13. Paneer Tikka Masala

Paneer Tikka Masala is a classic Indian dish that is creamy, flavorful, and downright delicious! It is prepared with Indian cheese chunks called paneer, cooked in a spicy gravy with a variety of herbs and spices.
Serving: 4
Preparation time: 15 minutes
Ready time: 30 minutes

Ingredients:
- 250g cubed paneer
- 2 chopped onions
- 2 chopped tomatoes
- 2 tbsps Kashmiri chilli powder
- 1 tsp garam masala powder
- 1/2 tsp turmeric powder
- 2 tbsps vegetable oil
- 2 tbsps cream
- 1/4 cup chopped coriander

- Salt to taste

Instructions:
1. Heat the oil in a pan over medium-high heat.
2. Add the onions and fry for 3-4 minutes.
3. Add the tomatoes, chilli powder, garam masala, turmeric powder, and salt. Fry for 5-6 minutes.
4. Add the paneer and mix until well combined.
5. Reduce the heat to low and add the cream. Cook for 8-10 minutes, stirring occasionally.
6. Garnish with chopped coriander and serve.

Nutrition information:
Calories- 340 kcal
Protein- 16g
Carbs- 18g
Fat- 24g

14. Chicken Biryani

Chicken Biryani is a classic Indian dish that combines aromatic spices with chicken and long-grained basmati rice, cooked in a flavorful broth.
Serving: This recipe makes 4 – 6 servings.
Preparation time: 20 minutes
Ready Time: 50 minutes

Ingredients:
- 2 tablespoons cooking oil
- 2 teaspoons cumin seeds
- 4 green cardamom pods
- 10 black peppercorns
- 1 small cinnamon stick
- 2 bay leaves
- 1 large onion, finely chopped
- 2 cloves garlic, grated
- 2 teaspoons finely grated ginger
- 1 teaspoon freshly ground turmeric powder
- 2 teaspoon garam masala

- 2 lbs. boneless, skinless chicken thighs, cut into 1-inch pieces
- 1 teaspoon salt
- 2 cups basmati rice, rinsed and drained
- 1/2 cup plain yogurt
- 2 cups chicken broth
- 2 tablespoons fresh cilantro, chopped
- 1 tablespoon fresh mint, chopped

Instructions:
1. Heat the oil in a large saucepan over medium heat. Add the cumin seeds, cardamom, peppercorns, cinnamon and bay leaves and sauté for 1 minute.
2. Add the onion and fry until golden brown. Add the garlic and ginger and stir-fry for another minute.
3. Add the turmeric and garam masala and fry for 1 minute more.
4. Add the chicken, salt and rice and stir-fry for a few minutes.
5. Add the yogurt and chicken broth and reduce the heat to a simmer.Cover and cook for 25 minutes, or until the rice is cooked and the chicken is tender.
6. Uncover and fluff up the rice with a fork. Garnish with cilantro and mint and serve hot.

Nutrition information
This dish contains about 600 calories per serving. It is also high in protein, carbohydrates and fiber.

15. Baingan Bharta

Baingan Bharta is an Indian classic dish made of roasted eggplant mashed together with tomatoes, onions, and spices. It is an easy and delicious vegan dish that anyone can enjoy.
Serving: 4
Preparation time: 15 minutes
Ready Time:30 minutes

Ingredients:
-1 large eggplant
-1 onion, chopped

-2 tomatoes, chopped
-1/2 teaspoon ground cumin
-1/4 teaspoon ground coriander
-1/4 teaspoon chili powder
-1 teaspoon garam masala
-2 tablespoon oil
-Salt and pepper to taste

Instructions:
1. Preheat oven to 350 degrees Fahrenheit.
2. Cut the eggplant in half and place on a baking sheet.
3. Bake until the eggplant is tender and roasted - about 25 minutes
4. Remove the eggplant from the oven and allow it to cool.
5. Peel off the skin of the eggplant and discard.
6. Mash the remaining pulp in a bowl.
7. Heat oil in a pan over medium-high heat and add the chopped onion. Sauté until the onion is soft and translucent.
8. Add the mashed eggplant to the pan and stir to combine with the onion.
9. Add the chopped tomatoes, cumin, coriander, chili powder, and garam masala and stir to combine.
10. Cook until the tomatoes are softened - about 5 minutes.
11. Season with salt and pepper to taste.
12. Serve warm.

Nutrition information: Per serving - Calories: 64, Total Fat:6 g, Saturated Fat: 0 g, Cholesterol: 0 mg, Sodium: 40 mg, Total Carbohydrates: 6 g, Dietary Fiber: 2 g, Sugars: 3 g, Protein: 1g.

16. Goat Curry

Goat Curry is a delicious and hearty dish featuring pieces of goat meat cooked in a flavorful sauce. The curry is a great meal to serve when you have guests as it is easily customizable.
Serving: 8
Preparation time: 10 minutes
Ready time: 2 hours

Ingredients:
- 2 lbs of goat meat, cut into chunks
- 3 tablespoons of olive oil
- 2 onions, finely chopped
- 4 cloves of garlic, minced
- 2 teaspoons of ground cumin
- 2 teaspoons of ground coriander
- 1 teaspoon of ground turmeric
- 2 tablespoons of tomato paste
- 1 (14 ounce) can of coconut milk
- 1 teaspoon of garam masala
- 2 tablespoons of freshly chopped cilantro
- Salt and freshly ground black pepper to taste

Instructions:
1. Heat the olive oil in a large skillet over medium-high heat. Add the goat meat and cook for 10 minutes, or until lightly browned.
2. Add the onions and garlic to the skillet and cook for 5 minutes, or until softened.
3. Add the cumin, coriander, and turmeric to the skillet and cook for 1 minute.
4. Add the tomato paste and coconut milk to the skillet and reduce the heat to low. Simmer for 1 hour, stirring occasionally.
5. Add the garam masala and cilantro to the skillet and stir to combine. Simmer for an additional 30 minutes, stirring occasionally.
6. Season with salt and pepper to taste. Serve hot.

Nutrition information:
Calories: 345, Fat: 23g, Cholesterol: 75mg, Sodium: 210mg, Carbohydrates: 4g, Fiber: 1g, Protein: 28g

17. Rajma Masala

Rajma Masala is a North Indian dish consisting of red kidney beans cooked in an aromatic and mildly spiced onion and tomato gravy.
Serving: 6-8 serviings
Preparation Time: 30 minutes
Ready Time: 2-3 hours

Ingredients:
2 cups red kidney beans (rajma)
2 tablespoons oil
1 teaspoon cumin seeds (jeera)
2 medium onions, finely chopped
2 tomatoes, finely chopped
1 teaspoon ginger-garlic paste
2 teaspoons coriander powder
1 teaspoon garam masala
2 green chillies, chopped
1 teaspoon chilli powder
Salt, to taste
1 tablespoon fresh coriander leaves, finely chopped

Instructions:
1. Soak the red kidney beans (rajma) overnight in enough water.
2. Drain and rinse the soaked rajma and pressure cook it with 2 cups of water and 1/2 teaspoon of salt for 2-3 whistles until the beans are soft and well cooked.
3. Heat oil in a pan on medium flame.
4. Add cumin seed, let it sizzle.
5. Add the chopped onions and fry till they become golden.
6. Add ginger-garlic paste and fry for few more minutes.
7. Add chopped tomatoes and cook till they become mushy.
8. Add coriander powder, garam masala, chilli powder and salt and mix well.
9. Add the cooked rajma and mix well.
10. Add a cup of water and let it simmer for 10-15 minutes or till the desired gravy thickness is achieved.
11. Finally garnish with fresh coriander leaves.

Nutrition information:
Calories: 175 kcal, Carbohydrates: 30 g, Protein: 10 g, Fat: 3 g, Saturated Fat: 0.5 g, Sodium: 351 mg, Potassium: 440 mg, Fiber: 10 g, Sugar: 6 g, Vitamin A: 565 IU, Vitamin C: 27 mg, Calcium: 61 mg, Iron: 4.3 mg

18. Vegetable Pulao

Vegetable Pulao is a flavorful and aromatic rice dish loaded with vegetables. It is a great one pot meal that is easy to make and very nutritious.
Serving: 4
Preparation Time: 10 minutes
Ready Time: 25 minutes

Ingredients:
- 1 tablespoon oil
- 2 teaspoons cumin
- 1 teaspoon mustard seeds
- Pinch of asafoetida
- 1 large onion, finely chopped
- 2 cups cooked rice
- 2 carrots, grated
- 1 cup peas
- ½ cup french beans, cut into small pieces
- Salt to taste
- ½ teaspoon garam masala
- 2 tablespoons freshly chopped coriander

Instructions:
1. Heat oil in a skillet over medium heat for a minute.
2. Add cumin, mustard seeds and asafoetida. Allow the spices to sizzle for 30 seconds.
3. Add the onion, and cook until lightly browned, about 4 minutes.
4. Add the carrots, peas, and french beans, and cook for 2 minutes, stirring occasionally.
5. Add the cooked rice and salt and stir everything together.
6. Add the garam masala and coriander, and mix well.
7. Cook for an additional 5 minutes, stirring occasionally.
8. Serve the Vegetable Pulao warm with your favorite accompaniments.

Nutrition information:
Per Serving: 265 calories, 8 g fat, 45 g carbohydrates, 5 g protein

19. Chicken Korma

Chicken Korma is a savory, mild, and creamy Indian dish that is perfect for dinner or an appetizer.
Serving: Serves 4 people.
Preparation Time: 10 minutes
Ready in: 45 minutes

Ingredients:
- 2 tablespoons of vegetable oil
- 1 onion, diced
- 2 big cloves of garlic, minced
- 1 teaspoon of grated ginger
- 1 teaspoon of ground cardamom
- 1 teaspoon of ground cinnamon
- 1 teaspoon of garam masala
- ½ cup of plain Greek yogurt
- 1 tablespoon of tomato paste
- 4 boneless, skinless chicken thighs, cubed
- 1 cup of chicken broth
- 2 tablespoons of sliced almonds
- 2 tablespoons of golden raisins

Instructions:
1. Heat the vegetable oil on medium in a large pan.
2. Add the onions and cook for 5 minutes, stirring occasionally.
3. Add the garlic and ginger and cook for 1 minute, stirring constantly.
4. Add the cardamom, cinnamon, and garam masala and stir for another minute.
5. Add the yogurt, tomato paste, chicken cubes, chicken broth, almonds, and raisins and stir until combined.
6. Reduce heat to low and simmer for 30 minutes or until the chicken is cooked through.
7. Serve over rice or couscous.

Nutrition information:
Calories: 270
Total Fat: 9g
Saturated Fat: 2.5g
Cholesterol: 55mg

Sodium: 450mg
Total Carbohydrates: 24g
Dietary Fiber: 2g
Sugars: 10g
Protein: 16g

20. Malai Kofta

Malai Kofta is a delicious dish made with deep-fried mashed potato dumplings that are simmered in a creamy, spiced tomato-onion sauce.
Serving: 6
Preparation Time: 20 minutes
Ready Time: 35 minutes

Ingredients:
- 2 large potatoes (boiled and mashed)
- 1/2 cup paneer (grated)
- 2 tablespoons cornflour
- 2 tablespoons chopped cashews
- 1 teaspoon cumin seeds
- 2 tablespoons raisins
- 1 tablespoon grated ginger
- 2 tablespoons chopped coriander
- 1 teaspoon garam masala
- Salt and pepper to taste
- Oil for shallow frying

For the Sauce:
- 2 tablespoons oil
- 1 small onion (finely chopped)
- 1 teaspoon ginger-garlic paste
- 2 tomatoes (blended)
- 2 teaspoons coriander powder
- 1 teaspoon cumin powder
- 1 teaspoon garam masala
- Salt to taste
- 2 tablespoons cream

Instructions:

1. In a bowl, add mashed potatoes, grated paneer, cornflour, cashews, cumin seeds, raisins, ginger, coriander, garam masala, salt, and pepper. Knead everything together into a dough.
2. Divide the dough into 12 balls and flatten them. Heat oil in a shallow frying pan and fry the flattened balls until they are lightly golden.
3. To make the sauce, heat oil in a pan and add the finely chopped onion. Fry until lightly golden, then add the ginger-garlic paste.
4. Add the blended tomatoes and stir fry for five minutes. Add the coriander and cumin powders, garam masala, salt, and cream.
5. Simmer for five minutes, then add the koftas to the pan. Simmer for a further 5 minutes, stirring occasionally.
6. Serve hot with garlic naan or roti and chopped coriander as a garnish.

Nutrition information: 205 calories, 10.3 g fat, 8.2 g protein, 18.7 g carbohydrates, 2.8 g fiber, 11 mg sodium.

21. Prawn Curry

Prawn curry is an incredibly flavorful and mouth-watering dish from Indian and South Asian cuisine. It's a traditional dish that has been served for generations at various celebrations and family gatherings. It's made with succulent prawns simmered in a flavorful curry sauce.
Serving: 6-8
Preparation Time: 15 minutes
Ready Time: 30 minutes

Ingredients:
- 1 lb prawns (about 20-24), peeled and deveined, tails removed
- 2 tablespoons canola oil
- 1 onion, diced
- 1 tablespoon minced garlic
- 1 tablespoon grated ginger
- 2 tablespoons curry powder
- ½ teaspoon ground black pepper
- 1 ½ teaspoon ground cumin
- 1 teaspoon ground turmeric
- 2 teaspoons garam masala
- 1 teaspoon chili powder

- 1 (14.5-ounce) can fire-roasted diced tomatoes
- 1 ½ cups vegetable broth
- 2 tablespoons freshly chopped cilantro
- Salt, to taste

Instructions:
1. Heat the oil in a large saucepan over medium-high heat.
2. Once the oil is hot, add the onion and cook for 2 minutes, stirring occasionally.
3. Add the garlic, ginger, curry powder, black pepper, cumin, turmeric, garam masala, and chili powder. Cook for 2 minutes, stirring occasionally.
4. Add the tomatoes and broth. Bring to a boil, reduce the heat to medium, and simmer for 10 minutes.
5. Add the prawns and cook for 3 minutes, or until pink and cooked through.
6. Stir in the cilantro and season with salt, to taste.
7. Serve Immediately.

Nutrition information: Per serving (1/6 of recipe): Calories: 214, Fat: 11.3g, Carbs: 9.4g, Protein: 18.7g, Fiber: 2.8g, Sodium: 503mg

22. Aloo Palak

Aloo Palak is an Indian vegetarian dish with potatoes as its main base ingredient. The dish is usually served with Indian flatbreads, rice, or any various types of fried bread.

Serving: 4
Preparation Time: 10 minutes
Ready Time: 25 minutes

Ingredients:
- 1 large onion, chopped
- 2 teaspoons cumin
- 2 tablespoons canola oil
- 4 cloves garlic, minced
- 1/2 teaspoon turmeric
- 1/2 teaspoon cayenne pepper

- 3 cups spinach, washed and chopped
- 1 teaspoon ground coriander
- 1 teaspoon ground cumin
- 4 medium potatoes, peeled and cubed
- 2 cups water

Instructions:
1. In a large pot, add the onion and cumin and sauté in the oil until the onions are translucent.
2. Add the garlic and spices and stir-fry for 1 minute.
3. Add the spinach, potatoes and water to the pot. Stir to combine.
4. Cover and bring to a boil. Lower the heat and simmer for 15 minutes or until the potatoes are tender.
5. Serve hot with flatbreads, rice or any type of fried bread.

Nutrition information: 506 calories, 16 g fat, 83 g carbohydrates, 11 g protein

23. Pork Vindaloo

Pork Vindaloo is a tangy, spicy Indian curry dish. Popular in Goa and South India, this dish is now widely available globally.
Serving: 4
Preparation time: 15 minutes
Ready time: 1 hour

Ingredients:
- 2 lbs pork shoulder, diced into 1-inch cubes
- 5 tablespoons vegetable oil
- 2 tablespoons fresh minced garlic
- 2 teaspoons ground cumin
- 2 teaspoons ground coriander
- 2 teaspoons ground turmeric
- 1 teaspoon cayenne pepper
- 2 tablespoons fresh minced ginger
- 1 cup diced onion
- 2 tablespoons tomato paste
- 1 can (14 oz) diced tomatoes

- 2 tablespoons white vinegar
- 1/2 cup water
- Salt to taste

Instructions:
1. Heat the oil in a large pot over medium heat. Add garlic, cumin, coriander, turmeric, and cayenne pepper. Cook and stir for 1 minute.
2. Add pork cubes, stirring to coat with the spice mixture. Cook and stir until lightly browned, about 5 minutes.
3. Add the ginger, onion, and tomato paste. Cook and stir for 2 minutes.
4. Add the tomatoes, vinegar, and water. Bring to a boil, then reduce the heat to low. Simmer uncovered for 45 minutes, stirring occasionally.
5. Taste and add salt as necessary. Simmer an additional 10 minutes.

Nutrition information: Calories: 476, Fat: 26 g, Carbohydrates: 13 g, Protein: 42 g, Sodium: 616 mg

24. Masoor Dal

Masoor Dal is a dish made primarily with red lentils cooked in an onion-tomato masala. The dish is popular in India and many parts of South Asia.
Serving: 4
Preparation time: 10 minutes
Ready Time: 40 minutes

Ingredients:
- 1 cup red lentils
- 1 onion, finely chopped
- 2 tomatoes, finely chopped
- 2 green chillies, finely chopped
- 1 teaspoon cumin seeds
- 1 teaspoon turmeric powder
- 2 tablespoons ghee or oil
- Salt to taste
- 1 teaspoon garam masala
- 2 cloves garlic, finely chopped
- 2 tablespoons chopped coriander leaves

Instructions:
1. Rinse the lentils thoroughly in cold water and then soak them in water for 10 minutes.
2. Heat the ghee or oil in a deep pan over medium heat. Add the cumin seeds and let them crackle.
3. Add the onions and fry until they are golden brown.
4. Add the tomatoes, green chillies, garlic and fry for 2 minutes.
5. Add the turmeric powder, salt and fry for another 1 minute.
6. Add the lentils and 2 cups of water. Bring this to a boil and then reduce the heat to low. Cover the pan and cook for 20 minutes or until the lentils are tender.
7. Add the garam masala and mix it in. Cook for 3-4 minutes more.
8. Remove from heat and garnish with coriander leaves.

Nutrition information:
One serving of Masoor Dal provides approximately 119 calories, 2 grams of fat, 19 grams of carbohydrates, and 8 grams of protein. It also provides a good amount of dietary fiber, phosphorus, and iron.

25. Fish Biryani

Fish Biryani is an aromatic and flavorful rice dish that consists of spiced fish, basmati rice, yogurt, and a variety of aromatic spices. This dish is popular in India and typically served as a main course.
Serving: 4-6
Preparation time: 20 minutes
Ready time: 1 hour

Ingredients:
- 1 cup Basmati rice
- 1 lb. fish fillets, cut into cubes
- 1 teaspoon turmeric powder
- 2 tablespoons ginger-garlic paste
- 2 tablespoons oil
- 2 onions, thinly sliced
- 1 teaspoon cumin seeds
- 2 tablespoons coriander powder

- Salt to taste
- 2 [cups] yogurt
- 1 teaspoon red chili powder
- 2 tablespoons garam masala powder
- 2 tablespoons chopped fresh cilantro leaves

Instructions:
1. Soak the Basmati rice in cold water, for 15-20 minutes.
2. In a bowl, mix together the fish cubes with turmeric, ginger-garlic paste, and a pinch of salt.
3. Heat the oil in a deep-bottomed pan. Add the onion slices and fry till golden brown.
4. Add the cumin seeds and fry for a few seconds.
5. Add the fish cubes, coriander powder, and salt. Fry for 3-4 minutes.
6. Drain the rice and add it to the pan. Mix to combine.
7. Add the yogurt, red chili powder, and garam masala. Mix to combine.
8. Cook covered on low heat for 25-30 minutes.
9. Garnish with fresh coriander leaves and serve hot.

Nutrition information:
Calories: 343, Fat: 11g, Protein: 28g, Carbohydrates: 34g, Fiber: 1g, Sugar: 3g

26. Mushroom Matar

Mushroom Matar is a dish made of mushrooms and fresh peas in a rich sauce. It is flavorful Indian-style curry dish.
Serving: 4
Preparation Time: 10 minutes
Ready Time: 30 minutes

Ingredients:
- 2 tablespoons vegetable oil
- 2 cloves garlic, minced
- 1 teaspoon ground cumin
- 1 teaspoon ground turmeric
- 2 teaspoons garam masala
- 1 teaspoon red chili powder

- 1 onion, chopped
- 3/4 cup chopped tomato
- 2 cups mushrooms, sliced
- 2 cups fresh or frozen peas
- 1/4 cup plain yogurt
- Salt and freshly ground black pepper to taste

Instructions:
1. Heat oil in a large skillet over medium heat.
2. Add garlic, cumin, turmeric, garam masala, and chili powder, and cook until fragrant, about 1 minute.
3. Add onion and cook until softened, about 3 minutes.
4. Add tomato, mushrooms, and peas, and cook until vegetables are tender, about 10 minutes.
5. Reduce heat to low and stir in yogurt.
6. Simmer gently until sauce has thickened, about 10 minutes.
7. Season with salt and pepper, and serve hot.

Nutrition information:
Calories: 160 kcal, Protein: 8.2 g, Fat: 8.6 g, Carbs: 13.5 g, Fiber: 3.6 g, Sugar: 4.9 g

27. Mutton Curry

Mutton Curry is a popular dish from South Asia, typically prepared with slow-cooked lamb or goat in a flavorful and robustly spiced gravy.
Serving: 4-6
Preparation Time: 20 minutes
Ready Time: 1 hour 20 minutes

Ingredients:
- 2 tablespoons of ghee or vegetable oil
- 1 large onion, finely chopped
- 1 teaspoon of freshly grated ginger
- 1 teaspoon of garlic paste
- 1 teaspoon of coriander powder
- 1 teaspoon of cumin powder
- 2 tablespoons of garam masala

- 2 tablespoons of chili powder (optional)
- 2 pounds of mutton, cubed
- 2 large tomatoes, chopped
- 2 green chillies, finely chopped
- 1 teaspoon of turmeric powder
- 1 cup of yogurt
- Salt to taste

Instructions:
1. Heat the ghee or oil in a large pot over medium heat.
2. Add the onions and sauté for 3-4 minutes, until they are golden and fragrant.
3. Add the ginger and garlic paste and sauté for another minute.
4. Add the coriander, cumin, garam masala and chili powder and stir to combine.
5. Add the mutton cubes and stir to combine. Cook over medium high heat for 10 minutes.
6. Add the tomatoes, chillies, and turmeric powder and stir to combine. Cook for another 10 minutes.
7. Add the yogurt and stir to combine. Simmer over low heat, stirring occasionally, for 30 minutes.
8. Season with salt to taste, then serve.

Nutrition information: Per serving: 32g of fat, 418 kcal, 24g of protein.

28. Black-eyed Pea Curry

Black-eyed Pea Curry is a spicy and flavorful Indian curry dish with black-eyed peas, onions, and tomatoes as the main Ingredients.
Serving: 4
Preparation Time: 20 minutes
Ready Time: 30 minutes

Ingredients:
- 2 tablespoons vegetable oil
- 1 ½ cups chopped onion
- 2 tablespoons finely minced garlic

- 2 tablespoons ginger paste
- 2 cups cooked black-eyed peas
- 1 teaspoon ground cumin
- 1 teaspoon ground coriander
- 1 teaspoon turmeric
- 1 teaspoon ground cardamom
- ½ teaspoon cayenne pepper
- 1 can (16 ounce) diced tomatoes
- 2 tablespoons chopped fresh cilantro
- Salt and ground black pepper, to taste

Instructions:
1. Heat the oil in a medium-sized skillet over medium heat.
2. Add the onion and cook for 5 minutes, stirring often.
3. Add the garlic and ginger paste and cook for 1 minute, stirring constantly.
4. Add the black-eyed peas, cumin, coriander, turmeric, cardamom, and cayenne pepper. Stir to combine.
5. Add the tomatoes and stir to combine.
6. Reduce the heat to low and simmer for 15 minutes, stirring occasionally.
7. Add in the cilantro and season with salt and pepper to taste.
8. Serve over basmati rice or with warm flatbread or naan.

Nutrition information:
Calories: 297,
Fat: 7g,
Carbohydrates: 43g,
Protein: 14g,
Sodium: 425mg

29. Jeera Rice

Jeera Rice is an aromatic, flavourful and easy-to-make Indian dish made with Basmati rice, cumin and spices.
Serving: 4
Preparation Time: 10 minutes
Ready Time: 30 minutes

Ingredients:
- 2 cups Basmati Rice
- 2 tablespoons clarified butter
- 2 tablespoons Jeera (Cumin Seeds)
- 2 Bay Leaves
- 5 Green Cardamom
- 2 Black Cardamom
- 7-8 Cloves
- 5-6 Small Pieces of Cinnamon
- 1 teaspoon Salt

Instructions:
1. Wash the Basmati rice and keep aside.
2. Heat the clarified butter in a pressure cooker and add all the whole spices (Jeera, Bay Leaves, Green Cardamom, Black Cardamom, Cloves, Cinnamon)
3. Add the washed rice and sauté for two minutes.
4. Add two cups of water and salt.
5. Close the lid and cook the rice on a low flame for three to four whistles.
6. Once the pressure is released, fluff up the rice and serve hot with your favourite accompaniment.

Nutrition information: per serving (4): Calories: 442, Fat: 17.7g, Protein: 9.6g, Carbohydrates: 62.4g, Fiber: 2.2g, Sugar: 1.6g.

30. Chicken Curry

This recipe for Chicken Curry is a fragrant and flavorful dish that is sure to please! Combining a blend of aromatic spices, onion, garlic, tomato, and chicken, this dish is sure to be a hit.
Serving: 4
Preparation Time: 10 minutes
Ready Time: 30 minutes

Ingredients:
- 2 tablespoons vegetable oil

- 1 onion, diced
- 2 garlic cloves, minced
- 2-3 tablespoons curry powder
- 2 tablespoons tomato paste
- 1 teaspoon ground ginger
- 1/2 teaspoon ground cumin
- 1 teaspoon ground turmeric
- 1 pound boneless, skinless chicken breasts, cubed
- 1/2 cup chicken broth
- 1 (14.5 ounce) can diced tomatoes
- 1/2 cup coconut milk
- Salt and pepper to taste

Instructions:
1. Heat the oil in a large skillet over medium heat. Add the onion and garlic, and cook until the onion is softened, about 5 minutes.
2. Add the curry powder, tomato paste, ginger, cumin, and turmeric, and cook until the mixture is aromatic, about 1 minute.
3. Add the chicken and cook until browned, about 5 minutes.
4. Add the chicken broth, diced tomatoes, and coconut milk. Increase the heat to high and bring the mixture to a boil.
5. Reduce the heat to low and simmer until the chicken is cooked through and the sauce has thickened, about 15 minutes. Season with salt and pepper to taste.

Nutrition information:
Calories: 360, Fat: 15g, Saturated Fat: 8g, Carbohydrates: 15g, Fiber: 3g, Protein: 38g, Cholesterol: 90mg, Sodium: 296mg

31. Mixed Vegetable Curry

Mixed Vegetable Curry is a flavorful Indian dish that is made with a combination of vegetables, herbs, and spices. Served over hot basmati rice, it makes a delicious and simple dinner option.
Serving: 6
Preparation Time: 10 minutes
Ready Time: 25 minutes

Ingredients:
- 1 tablespoon vegetable oil
- 1 onion, diced
- 2 cloves garlic, minced
- 2 teaspoons grated ginger
- 1 teaspoon ground cumin
- 1 teaspoon ground coriander
- 1 teaspoon ground turmeric
- 1 teaspoon garam masala
- 1/2 teaspoon salt
- 2 large tomatoes, chopped
- 2 cups cauliflower florets
- 2 carrots, peeled and chopped
- 1 red bell pepper, chopped
- 1/2 cup frozen peas
- 1/2 cup vegetable broth
- 1/4 cup coconut milk

Instructions:
1. Heat the oil in a large skillet over medium heat. Add the onion and garlic and sauté for 3-4 minutes, until the onion is translucent.
2. Stir in the ginger, cumin, coriander, turmeric, garam masala, and salt, and cook until fragrant, about 1 minute.
3. Add the tomatoes, stir to combine, and cook for 1 minute.
4. Add the cauliflower, carrots, bell pepper, and frozen peas to the skillet. Stir to combine and cook for 3-4 minutes.
5. Add the vegetable broth and coconut milk and bring to a simmer. Cover and cook for 10 minutes, until the vegetables are tender.
6. Serve over hot basmati rice.

Nutrition information: Calories: 140, Total Fat: 5g, Saturated Fat: 3g, Trans Fat: 0g, Cholesterol: 0mg, Sodium: 293mg, Total Carbohydrates: 20g, Dietary Fiber: 5g, Sugars: 8g, Protein: 4g.

32. Chicken Jalfrezi

Chicken Jalfrezi is an easy-to-make, delicious and flavourful Indian dish that is sure to impress your guests. This healthy and tasty curry is made

with bite-sized pieces of chicken cooked with a variety of spices in a tangy tomato and onion gravy.
Serving: 6-8 people
Preparation time: 30 mins
Ready time: 45 mins

Ingredients:
1 pound chicken breast (cut into cubes)
3 tablespoons oil
1 teaspoon cumin seeds
1 large onion (finely chopped)
2 cloves garlic (minced)
1 teaspoon ground ginger
1 teaspoon ground coriander
1 teaspoon ground cumin
1 teaspoon salt
1 teaspoon ground turmeric
1 teaspoon black pepper
1 teaspoon garam masala
1 green chilies (chopped)
1 cup canned tomatoes (chopped)
1 cup chopped bell pepper (red and green)
2 tablespoons fresh lime juice
3 tablespoons chopped cilantro

Instructions:
1. Heat the oil in a large saucepan over medium heat. Once the oil is hot, add the cumin seeds and fry for one minute.
2. Add the chopped onion and fry until it starts to brown, about 5 minutes.
3. Add the minced garlic, ginger, coriander, cumin, salt, turmeric, black pepper, and garam masala. Cook for 1-2 minutes, stirring frequently.
4. Add the chicken cubes and stir to coat with the spices. Cook for another 5 minutes, stirring occasionally.
5. Add the chopped tomatoes, bell pepper and green chilies. Cover and cook for 15 minutes, stirring occasionally.
6. Add the lime juice and cilantro and stir to combine. Simmer for another 5 minutes uncovered or until the sauce reaches the desired consistency.

Nutrition information:
Calories - 270
Fat - 11g
Protein - 28g
Carbohydrates - 11g
Fiber - 2g

33. Vegetable Biryani

Vegetable biryani is a fragrant and flavorful Indian dish, combining cooked vegetables with rice, aromatic spices, and herbs.
Serving: 6
Preparation time: 20 minutes
Ready time: 45 minutes

Ingredients:
- 2 cups basmati rice
- 1 cup mixed vegetables (e.g. potatoes, carrots, peas, corn)
- 2 tablespoons ghee
- 1 onion, diced
- 3 cloves garlic, minced
- 1 inch ginger, grated
- 1 teaspoon cumin seeds
- 1 teaspoon garam masala
- 3 black cardamom pods
- 1 teaspoon turmeric
- 1 cup water
- 1/4 cup cilantro, finely chopped
- Salt and pepper to taste

Instructions:
1. Soak basmati rice in cold water for 20 minutes.
2. Heat ghee in a pan over medium heat and fry onions, garlic and ginger until fragrant and golden.
3. Add in cumin seeds, garam masala, cardamom pods, and turmeric and stir to combine.
4. Add mixed vegetables and stir to coat with spice mixture.
5. Add in rice and mix thoroughly.

6. Pour in water and season with salt and pepper.
7. Bring to a boil, reduce heat, cover and simmer for 15 minutes.
8. Add in cilantro and stir to combine.
9. Turn off heat and let biryani steam for 10 minutes before serving.

Nutrition information: Per Serving: 310 calories; 10 g fat; 41 g carbohydrate; 6 g protein; 3 g fiber.

34. Shahi Paneer

Shahi paneer is a creamy and rich North Indian dish made from paneer cubes and a delicious gravy prepared with Indian spices. It is always a great dish to serve at any special occasion or even on a regular day with hot Rotis or Naans.
Serving: 4
Preparation Time: 10 minutes
Ready Time: 30 minutes

Ingredients:
- 400g paneer, cubed
- 2 tablespoons oil
- 2 teaspoons cumin seeds
- 1 teaspoon finely chopped ginger
- 2 large tomatoes, chopped
- 2 tablespoons cream
- 2 tablespoons tomato paste
- 2 tablespoons chopped dried fenugreek leaves
- 2 green chillies, chopped
- ¼ teaspoon turmeric powder
- ½ teaspoon red chilli powder
- 1 teaspoon garam masala powder
- 1 teaspoon sugar
- Salt to taste

Instructions:
1. Heat oil in a pan and add the cumin seeds.
2. When they start to crackle, add the chopped ginger and sauté for a minute.

3. Now add the chopped tomatoes and sauté till they turn soft and pulpy.
4. Add the tomato paste, cream, fenugreek leaves, green chillies, turmeric powder, red chilli powder, garam masala powder, sugar and salt to the gravy and mix well.
5. Add the paneer cubes and mix gently.
6. Cover and cook the paneer gravy for about 10-15 minutes over medium heat, stirring occasionally.
7. Serve hot with naan or roti.

Nutrition information:
Calories: 243.5kcal,
Carbohydrates: 9.2g,
Protein: 10.6g,
Fat: 18.4g

35. Shrimp Curry

A zesty and flavor-packed shrimp curry dish that is appreciated everywhere, this classic Indian-inspired meal is simple to make and can be served with hot cooked basmati rice or soft flatbreads.
Serving: 4 to 6
Preparation Time: 10 minutes
Ready Time: 25 minutes

Ingredients:
- 2 tablespoons coconut oil or vegetable oil
- 1 large onion, chopped
- 1 large bell pepper, chopped
- 4 cups tomato sauce
- 2 tablespoons Madras-style curry powder
- 2 teaspoons ground cumin
- 1 teaspoon ground coriander
- Salt to taste
- 1½ pounds large shrimp, peeled and deveined
- 2 tablespoons unsweetened shredded coconut

Instructions:

1. Heat the oil in a medium skillet over medium-high heat. Add the onion and bell pepper and cook, stirring, for about 5 minutes, until the vegetables are softened.
2. Add the tomato sauce, curry powder, cumin, coriander, and salt and cook, stirring, for about 5 minutes, until the sauce is bubbling.
3. Add the shrimp and shredded coconut and cook, stirring, for about 5 minutes, until the shrimp are cooked through.
4. Serve the curry with hot cooked basmati rice or soft flatbreads.

Nutrition information:
Calories: 250, Fat: 8g, Protein: 22g, Fiber: 3g, Carbs: 30g, Sodium: 890mg

36. Aloo Matar

Aloo Matar is a flavorful Punjabi dish of potatoes and green peas simmered in a delicious tomato-based gravy.
Serving: 4
Preparation Time: 10 minutes
Ready Time: 40 minutes

Ingredients:
- 2 potatoes, cubed
- 1 cup green peas
- 1 onion, finely chopped
- 1 tomato, chopped
- 2 cloves garlic, finely chopped
- 1-inch piece ginger, grated
- 1 teaspoon cumin seeds
- 1 teaspoon coriander powder
- 1/2 teaspoon turmeric powder
- 1 teaspoon garam masala powder
- Salt, to taste
- 2 tablespoons vegetable oil
- 1 green chili, finely chopped

Instructions:
1. Heat oil in a pan.

2. Add cumin seeds, onion, garlic, ginger, and green chili, and fry until the onion turns golden.
3. Add tomatoes, coriander powder, turmeric powder, garam masala powder, and salt. Mix well and fry until the tomatoes are softened.
4. Add potatoes and green peas and cook, stirring occasionally, for 10 minutes.
5. Pour in a cup of water and stir to combine. Cover and simmer for 20-25 minutes, until the potatoes are cooked.
6. Uncover and simmer for 10 minutes more until the gravy has thickened.
7. Serve hot with steamed rice or chapati.

Nutrition information: Per serving: 302 calories, 16.3g fat, 34.5g carbohydrates, 5g protein.

37. Lamb Korma

Lamb Korma is an Indian curry dish made of lamb and a number of different spices and herbs. It is traditionally served with Indian bread or Indian rice.

Serving: 4
Preparation time: 10 minutes
Ready time: 25 minutes

Ingredients:
- 500g lean lamb, cut into cubes
- 2 onions, diced
- 2 cloves garlic, finely chopped
- 2 tsp ground coriander
- 2 tsp ground cumin
- 2 tsp garam masala
- 3 tsp ground turmeric
- 2 bay leaves
- 2 green chillies
- 1 can of coconut milk
- 2-3 tablespoons of vegetable oil
- 2 tablespoons of chopped coriander leaves
-Salt and pepper to taste

Instructions:
1. Heat the oil in a large saucepan over a medium heat.
2. Add the onions and fry, stirring regularly, until golden brown (for about 5 minutes).
3. Add the garlic and spices, and fry, stirring, for another 2 minutes.
4. Add the lamb and fry for another 5 minutes.
5. Pour the coconut milk into the pan with the lamb mixture and stir well.
6. Add the bay leaves and chillies, bring to the boil, then reduce the heat and simmer, covered, for about 20 minutes, stirring occasionally.
7. Taste and season with salt and pepper if desired.
8. Remove from the heat and stir in the chopped coriander leaves.

Nutrition information:
Serving size: 1 portion
Calories: 300
Fat: 20g
Carbohydrates: 10g
Protein: 15g

38. Dal Tadka

Dal Tadka is a classic Indian dish. It's made with yellow lentils and is simmered together with aromatic spices to make a delicious and satisfying one-pot meal.
Serving: Serves 4
Preparation time: 10 minutes
Ready Time: 30 minutes

Ingredients:
- 1 cup yellow lentils
- ½ tsp cumin
- ½ tsp coriander
- ½ tsp turmeric
- 1 tsp chili powder
- 1 onion, chopped
- 2 cloves garlic, minced

- 1 tsp ginger, minced
- 2 tomatoes, chopped
- 1 green chilli, chopped
- 1 tsp cumin seeds
- 2 tbsp ghee
- 2 cups water

Instructions:
1. Wash and rinse the lentils.
2. In a large pot, heat the ghee and add the cumin seeds.
3. Add the onion, garlic, ginger, chilli, tomatoes and stir for 2 minutes.
4. Add the lentils, cumin, coriander, turmeric, chilli powder and stir.
5. Add the water and bring to a boil.
6. Reduce the heat and simmer for 20 minutes until the lentils are tender.
7. Serve with steamed basmati rice and enjoy!

Nutrition information
Per Serving: Calories: 243, Total Fat: 9 g, Saturated Fat: 5 g, Polyunsaturated Fat: 1 g, Monounsaturated Fat: 1 g, Cholesterol: 20 mg, Sodium: 205 mg, Potassium: 582 mg, Carbohydrates: 32 g, Dietary Fiber: 12 g, Sugars: 4 g, Protein: 11 g.

39. Fish Korma

Fish Korma is an easy to make, fragrant and delicious Indian curry. It is a perfect combination of robust spices like turmeric, garam masala and fresh herbs.
Serving: 4
Preparation time: 15 mins
Ready time: 30 mins

Ingredients:
- 2 tablespoons of ghee, or oil
- 1 teaspoon of cumin seeds
- 2 large onions, finely chopped
- 2 green chillies, finely chopped
- 2 cloves of garlic, finely chopped
- 1 teaspoon of ground turmeric

- 2 teaspoons of garam masala
- 2 large tomatoes, finely chopped
- 250g (8oz) of firm white fish, cut into 2cm (1in) cubes
- 400ml (14floz) of coconut milk
- 2 tablespoons of freshly chopped coriander leaves

Instructions:
1. Heat the ghee or oil in a large pan over a medium heat.
2. Add the cumin seeds and cook for 1 minute until they start to sizzle.
3. Add the onions, chillies and garlic and cook for 5 minutes until the onions have softened.
4. Add the turmeric and garam masala and cook for 1 minute.
5. Add the tomatoes and fish and cook for a further 5 minutes.
6. Stir in the coconut milk and bring to a gentle simmer.
7. Simmer for 10 minutes until the fish is cooked through.
8. Stir in the coriander and serve.

Nutrition information: Per serving: 217kcal, Protein 17.5g, Carbohydrates 9.8g, Fat 11.5g, Saturated fat 6.3g, Fibre 4.2g, Sugar 2.8g, Salt 0.9g

40. Baingan Mirch Ka Salan

Baingan Mirch Ka Salan is an Indian vegetable dish made with eggplants and chili peppers cooked in a rich, spicy, and creamy gravy. Serve this flavorful dish with roti or rice for a delicious meal.
Serving: 4
Preparation Time: 15 minutes
Ready Time: 45 minutes

Ingredients:
· 3 large eggplants
· 2 tablespoons cooking oil
· 1 tablespoon cumin seeds
· 2-3 medium green chili peppers, diced
· 1 medium onion, diced
· 2 cloves garlic, diced
· 2 teaspoons coriander powder

- 1 teaspoon chili powder
- Salt to taste
- 2 medium tomatoes, diced
- 2 tablespoons fresh cilantro, chopped
- ½ cup water

Instructions:
1. Preheat the oven to 450°F. Slice the eggplants into rounds and place in a greased baking sheet. Bake for 25 minutes, or until the eggplants are tender. Remove from the oven and set aside.
2. In a large skillet, heat the cooking oil over medium-high heat. Add the cumin seeds and the diced chili peppers, onions and garlic, and sauté until the onions are golden-brown.
3. Add the coriander and chili powders and stir for one minute.
4. Add the diced tomatoes and the cooked eggplant slices to the skillet. Season with salt to taste and mix everything together.
5. Cook uncovered for 15 minutes, stirring occasionally, until the mixture is thick and creamy.
6. Just before serving, add the chopped cilantro and stir.
7. Serve hot with roti or rice.

Nutrition information:
Calories - 222,
Total fat - 9g,
Saturated fat - 1g,
Total carbohydrate - 31g,
Protein - 5g.

41. Keema Matar

Keema Matar is a delicious and hearty curry made with ground beef, green peas and a blend of Indian spices.
Serving: 6
Preparation Time: 10 minutes
Ready Time: 40 minutes

Ingredients:
- 1 lb ground beef

- 2 tablespoons cooking oil
- 1 teaspoon cumin seeds
- 2 cloves garlic, minced
- 1 teaspoon ground ginger
- 1 teaspoon ground coriander
- 1/2 teaspoon garam masala
- 1/2 teaspoon red chili powder
- 1/4 teaspoon turmeric powder
- 1 cup frozen green peas
- 2 tomatoes, chopped
- 1/4 cup water
- 1/2 teaspoon salt, or to taste

Instructions:

1. Heat oil in a large pan over medium heat. Add cumin seeds and garlic, and cook for 1 minute.
2. Add ground beef and stir-fry for 5 minutes, until the beef is lightly browned.
3. Add the ginger, coriander, garam masala, red chili powder, and turmeric, stirring to combine. Cook for 1 minute.
4. Add the frozen peas, tomatoes, and water. Give everything a good stir, cover, and reduce the heat to low. Simmer uncovered for 20 minutes, stirring occasionally.
5. Add the salt, stir to combine, and cook for an additional 5 minutes.

Nutrition information:

Per serving (Approximate): Calories: 329, Fat: 18 g, Protein: 23 g, Carbohydrates: 12 g.

42. Chole Bhature

Chole Bhature is a classic Punjabi dish featuring a spicy tomato based chickpea curry served with crisp fried bhaturas.
Serving: 2
Preparation Time: 10 minutes
Ready Time: 30 minutes

Ingredients:

- 1 can of chickpeas
- 1 large onion, finely chopped
- 2 green chillies, chopped
- 1 teaspoon of garam masala
- 2 tablespoons of oil
- 2 cups of all-purpose flour
- 1 tablespoon of baking powder
- 1 cup of plain yogurt
- 2 cups of warm water
- Salt, to taste

Instructions:
1. To make the chole, heat oil in a large pan over medium heat. Add the onions and fry for 2-3 minutes. Add garam masala, chillies, and salt and fry for a few more minutes.
2. Add the chickpeas, a cup of water and stir. Cover and simmer for 10-15 minutes.
3. In the meantime, make the bhaturas. In a bowl, mix the flour, baking powder, and salt. Add the yogurt and mix. Slowly add the water to make a soft dough.
4. Divide the dough into small portions and roll out each into thin, round shapes.
5. Heat some oil in a pan and fry the bhaturas until golden and crisp.

Nutrition information:
Calories: 948 kcal
Carbohydrates: 108 g
Protein: 28 g
Fat: 45 g
Saturated Fat: 9 g
Cholesterol: 58 mg
Sodium: 948 mg
Potassium: 1287 mg
Fiber: 16 g
Sugar: 16 g
Vitamin C: 28.5 mg
Calcium: 374 mg
Iron: 16.6 mg

43. Chicken Vindaloo

Chicken Vindaloo is a classic Indian curried dish, usually made with chicken thighs that are marinated and then cooked in a spicy and tangy Tomato-Vinegar based sauce.

Serving: 4-6
Preparation time: 20 minutes
Ready time: 45 minutes

Ingredients:
- 2 tablespoons of vegetable oil
- 2 large onions, finely chopped
- 6 cloves of garlic, minced
- 1 tablespoon of freshly grated ginger
- 1 teaspoon of ground cumin
- 1 teaspoon of ground coriander
- 1 teaspoon of ground turmeric
- 1 teaspoon of garam masala
- 1 teaspoon of cayenne pepper (optional)
- 1 tablespoon of tomato paste
- 1/2 cup of white vinegar
- 1/4 cup of water
- 4-6 boneless, skinless chicken thighs, cut into 1-inch cubes
- 1/2 cup of plain Greek yogurt
- 1/2 teaspoon of salt
- Juice of 1/2 lime

Instructions:
1. Heat the vegetable oil in a large skillet over medium heat. Add the onions, garlic, and ginger and cook until the onions are soft and golden brown, about 5 minutes.
2. Add the cumin, coriander, turmeric, garam masala, and cayenne pepper (if using) and cook for 1 minute.
3. Add the tomato paste and cook for 2 minutes.
4. Add the vinegar and water and bring to a boil.
5. Add the chicken cubes and cook until they are cooked through, about 10 minutes.
6. Add the yogurt, salt, and lime juice and stir to combine. Simmer for 10 minutes.
7. Serve over rice or with naan.

Nutrition information: 6 servings;
Total Calories: 250;
Total Fat: 10g;
Total Carbohydrate: 16g;
Protein: 24g;
Sodium: 400mg;
Fiber: 2g.

44. Paneer Butter Masala

Paneer Butter Masala is a delicious Indian dish that combines soft paneer cubes with a rich, creamy, and spiced tomato-based sauce.
Serving: 4-6
Preparation Time: 15 Minutes
Ready Time: 45 Minutes

Ingredients:
- 350g diced paneer
- 3 tablespoons vegetable oil
- 1 teaspoon whole cumin (jeera) seeds
- 2 large onions, finely chopped
- 1 tablespoon minced garlic
- 1 tablespoon minced ginger
- 2 teaspoons ground cumin (jeera)
- 1 teaspoon ground coriander
- 1/2 teaspoon garam masala
- 2 tomatoes, finely chopped
- 2 tablespoons butter
- 2 tablespoons cream
- Salt and pepper, to taste

Instructions:
1. Heat the oil in a large skillet or wok over medium heat.
2. Add the cumin and cook until it sizzles, then add the onions.
3. Sauté the onions until they are lightly browned.
4. Add the garlic and ginger and cook for a few minutes.

5. Add the ground cumin, coriander, and garam masala, stirring constantly.
6. Add the tomatoes and cook for another few minutes until the sauce thickens.
7. Add the paneer and stir to combine.
8. Add the butter and cream and simmer for a few minutes until the sauce is thick and creamy.
9. Add salt and pepper to taste.
10. Serve with rice or naan.

Nutrition information: Each serving has approximately 350 calories, 18g fat, 11g protein, and 22g carbohydrates.

45. Goat Biryani

Goat Biryani is a popular Indian dish made with succulent pieces of goat, basmati rice, and an array of aromatic spices. This wonderfully flavorful dish is sure to tantalize the taste buds.
Serving: 6-8
Preparation Time: 20 minutes
Ready Time: 1 hour

Ingredients:
- 1kg goat cubes, trimmed
- 2 cups basmati rice, rinsed
- 1 onion, finely chopped
- 4 cloves garlic, minced
- 2 teaspoons grated ginger
- 2 teaspoons garam masala
- 1 teaspoon chili powder
- 1 teaspoon cumin powder
- 1 teaspoon turmeric powder
- 1 teaspoon ground coriander
- 2 tablespoons oil
- 2 tablespoons plain yogurt
- 2 tablespoons chopped cilantro
- Salt, to taste
- 1 cup water or chicken broth

Instructions:
1. In a large bowl, combine the goat cubes, garlic, onion, ginger, garam masala, chili powder, cumin powder, turmeric powder, ground coriander, oil, plain yogurt, cilantro, and salt. Mix until all the Ingredients are well combined. Set aside.
2. Heat a large pot or dutch oven over medium-high heat. Add the marinated goat cubes to the pot and sauté for 8-10 minutes, stirring occasionally.
3. Add the rinsed basmati rice to the pot and stir until the rice is lightly toasted, about 2 minutes.
4. Add the water or chicken broth and bring the mixture to a boil. Reduce the heat to low, cover the pot, and cook for 15 minutes.
5. Turn off the heat and let the goat biryani sit for 10 minutes. Fluff the rice with a fork before serving.

Nutrition information:
Calories: 465, Fat: 17.3g, Saturated fat: 4g, Cholesterol: 97mg, Sodium: 395mg, Carbohydrates: 45.9g, Fiber: 6.2g, Protein: 30.5g.

46. Bhindi Masala

Bhindi Masala is a popular North Indian dish made with stir-fried okra and onions along with Indian spices. It is one of the most versatile side dishes and can be served with any main course from rotis to rice.
Serving: 4
Preparation Time: 15 minutes
Ready Time: 40 minutes

Ingredients:
- 2 cups okra/bhindi, sliced lengthwise
- 2 onions, chopped
- 2 tomatoes, chopped
- 2 green chillies, chopped
- 1 teaspoon cumin seeds
- 1 teaspoon coriander powder
- 1 teaspoon garam masala
- ½ teaspoon turmeric powder

- 2 tablespoons oil
- Salt to taste

Instructions:
1. Heat oil in a pan.
2. Add cumin seeds and let them splutter.
3. Add the chopped onions, tomatoes and green chillies and sauté for a few minutes until the onions become golden brown.
4. Add the okra, turmeric powder, coriander powder, garam masala and salt and mix it all together.
5. Cover the pan and let the bhindi cook for about 10-15 minutes until it is tender.
6. Once all the spices and veggies are cooked well, remove the pan from heat.
7. Serve hot with chapati or rice.

Nutrition information:
Each serving of Bhindi Masala contains approximately 200 calories. It is a good source of dietary fiber, iron, vitamin C, and calcium.

47. Pork Curry

This traditional pork curry is full of flavour and is an ideal dish for a family meal.
Serving: 4-5
Preparation Time: 20 minutes
Ready Time: 1 hour

Ingredients:
- 500 grams of pork
- 2 tablespoons of oil
- 2 tablespoons of curry powder
- 2 cloves of garlic
- 1 onion
- 1 teaspoon of cumin
- ½ teaspoon of chili powder
- 1 cup of chicken stock
- 1 can of coconut milk (400ml)

Instructions:
1. In a large pan, heat the oil over a medium heat and add the pork. Fry until the pork is lightly brown.
2. Finely chop the garlic and onion and add to the pan with the pork. Add the curry powder, cumin and chilli powder and combine all Ingredients together until all the pork is covered.
3. Pour in the chicken stock and bring to a gentle simmer. Cover the pan and allow to simmer.
4. Add the coconut milk and mix through with the other Ingredients. Allow to simmer for around 30 minutes or until the pork is cooked through.
5. Serve with warm rice.

Nutrition information: Per serving: 498 calories, 28.8 g fat, 27.6 g carbohydrates, 37.1 g protein, 5.7 g fiber

48. Masoor Pulao

Masoor Pulao is a comforting, mild-flavored rice and lentil dish that is sure to become a favorite in your family.
Serving: 4
Preparation time: 10 minutes
Ready time: 45 minutes

Ingredients:
1 cup brown lentils, sorted and rinsed
2 tablespoons olive oil
1 medium onion, chopped
1 teaspoon ground cumin
1 teaspoon ground cardamom
2 cups Basmati rice, sorted and rinsed
3 cups vegetable broth
1 teaspoon kosher salt

Instructions:
1. In a large pot over medium heat, heat the oil. Add the onion and cook until softened and lightly browned, about 5 minutes.

2. Add the cumin and cardamom and stir for 1 minute.
3. Add the rice, lentils, and broth, and bring to a boil.
4. Reduce the heat to low, cover, and simmer for 30 minutes.
5. Remove the pot from the heat and let it sit for 10 minutes. Fluff the rice with a fork and stir to combine.

Nutrition information:
Calories: 384, Fat: 7g, Carbohydrates: 68g, Protein: 10g, Fiber: 6g, Sodium: 780mg

49. Egg Biryani

Delicious and easy to make, Egg Biryani is a traditional Indian dish made from basmati rice layered with gravy, onions, tomatoes and hard boiled eggs. It is bursting with flavors of aromatic spices.
Serving: 6
Preparation Time: 45 minutes
Ready Time: 60 minutes

Ingredients:
- 2 cups Basmati Rice
- 4 boiled eggs
- 1 onion, chopped
- 3 cloves garlic, minced
- 1 tsp cumin seeds
- 1 tsp turmeric powder
- 2 green chilis
- 2 tomatoes, chopped
- 1 inch ginger, chopped
- 2 tbsp yogurt
- 2 tbsp ghee
- 2 bay leaves
- Salt to taste
- 1 tsp garam masala
- 1/2 cup fresh coriander leaves, finely chopped

Instructions:

1. Heat ghee in a pan and add cumin seeds. When the seeds begin to crackle, add garlic and ginger and sauté for a few seconds.
2. Add chopped onions and sauté until they turn golden brown.
3. Add chopped tomatoes and green chilies and cook until the tomatoes are soft.
4. Add turmeric powder, salt and garam masala and stir for a few minutes.
5. Now add yogurt and stir for a few minutes.
6. Add boiled eggs and stir gently.
7. Add the basmati rice and mix gently.
8. Add 3 cups of water and bay leaves and bring to a boil.
9. Reduce heat and simmer for 15 minutes or until the rice is cooked and the water is absorbed.
10. Garnish with coriander leaves and serve hot.

Nutrition information: Per serving: Calories 390, Total Fat 12g, Protein 10g, Total Carbohydrate 61g, Cholesterol 151mg, Sodium 691mg.

50. Mushroom Curry

Mushroom Curry is an Indian dish that is quickly cooked in a rich and creamy tomato sauce. It is a delicious and hearty vegetarian meal that is sure to please.
Serving: 6
Preparation Time: 30 minutes
Ready Time: 1 hour

Ingredients:
- 3 tablespoons vegetable oil
- 1 onion, finely diced
- 1 tablespoon grated fresh ginger
- 4 cloves garlic, minced
- 2 teaspoons ground cumin
- 2 teaspoons ground coriander
- 2 teaspoons garam masala
- 1 teaspoon ground turmeric
- 1/2 teaspoon of ground chilli powder

- 2 cups diced tomatoes
- 2 cup vegetable broth
- 2 cups sliced mushrooms
- 1 teaspoon sugar
- 1/2 cup cream
- Salt and pepper to taste

Instructions:
1. Heat the oil in a large saucepan over medium heat.
2. Add the onion, ginger and garlic and cook for 5 minutes, stirring occasionally.
3. Add the cumin, coriander, garam masala, turmeric and chilli powder and cook for 1 minute, stirring often.
4. Add the diced tomatoes, vegetable broth and mushrooms and bring to a simmer.
5. Simmer the curry for 30 minutes, stirring occasionally.
6. Add the sugar and cream and simmer for an additional 5 minutes, stirring often.
7. Season with salt and pepper to taste.
8. Serve the mushroom curry over rice.

Nutrition information:
Calories: 191 kcal
Fat: 14 g
Carbohydrates: 11 g
Protein: 4 g
Fiber: 2.4 g

51. Mutton Korma

Mutton Korma is a delicious and aromatic North Indian dish that consists of slow cooked mutton pieces in a creamy gravy of yoghurt, nuts and spices.
Serving: 6
Preparation Time: 20 minutes
Ready Time: 90 minutes

Ingredients:

- 1 Kg mutton pieces
- 2 onions, sliced
- 2 tbsps garlic and ginger paste
- 2 tbsps oil
- 1 cup yoghurt
- 1/2 cup ground cashews and almonds
- 1/2 tsp garam masala
- Salt to taste

Instructions:
1. Heat oil in a pan and add the sliced onions. Fry them until golden.
2. Add the ginger and garlic pastes and fry until fragrant.
3. Add the mutton pieces and fry for a few minutes, stirring constantly.
4. Add the yoghurt, ground nuts and spices and mix thoroughly.
5. Cover the pan and allow the dish to simmer for around 90 minutes, until the mutton pieces are cooked through and tender.
6. Serve hot with cooked basmati rice.

Nutrition information: Per Serving - 443 kcal, Protein - 19.3g, Carbohydrates - 10.8g, Fat - 34.8g.

52. Navratan Korma

Navratan Korma is a mild Mughlai curry cooked with nuts, fruits, and spices. It is creamy, sweet, abundant, and packed full of flavor!
Serving: 4-6
Preparation Time: 10 minutes
Ready Time: 1 hour

Ingredients:
- 1 onion, chopped
- 2 tomatoes, chopped
- 4 cloves garlic, chopped
- 2-3 green chillies, chopped
- 1 teaspoon ground turmeric
- 1 teaspoon garam masala
- 1 teaspoon cumin powder
- 1 teaspoon coriander powder

- 5-6 cashews, ground into a paste
- 2 tablespoons ghee
- ¼ cup oil
- 1 cup mixed vegetables (carrots, peas, beans, corn)
- 2 tablespoons dried fenugreek leaves
- 1 cup thick coconut milk
- Salt to taste
- 2 tablespoons chopped fresh cilantro

Instructions:
1. Heat the ghee and oil in a pan over medium heat.
2. Add the onion and sauté for a few minutes until lightly golden.
3. Add the garlic and green chillies and sauté for a few more minutes.
4. Add the tomatoes and cook until softened.
5. Then add the turmeric, garam masala, cumin powder and coriander powder, and stir to combine.
6. Add the cashew paste and mixed vegetables and stir to combine.
7. Add the fenugreek leaves and stir to combine.
8. Pour in the coconut milk and stir to combine.
9. Simmer for 15-20 minutes until the vegetables are cooked through.
10. Add salt to taste and stir to combine.
11. Garnish with chopped fresh cilantro and serve.

Nutrition information: 180 calories, 9 g fat, 16 g carbohydrates, 3 g protein, 2 g fiber, 190 mg sodium

53. Prawn Biryani

Prawn Biryani is a rice-based dish cooked with prawns, spices and Indian herbs. It is a delicious and flavorful dish that can be served for special occasions or regular family dinners.
Serving: 4 servings
Preparation time: 15 minutes
Ready time: 40 minutes

Ingredients:
1 lb prawns (~450 g), peeled and deveined
2 cups basmati rice (~500 g)

1 onion, sliced
1 teaspoon garlic, minced
1 tablespoon ginger, grated
½ teaspoon turmeric
1 teaspoon coriander powder
2 green chillies, finely chopped
2 tablespoons oil
4 tablespoons yogurt
½ teaspoon garam masala
½ teaspoon chilli powder
1 teaspoon salt

Instructions:
1. Wash the rice and soak it for 30 minutes.
2. Heat the oil in a large pot on medium heat. Add the onions and fry until golden brown.
3. Add garlic, ginger, turmeric, coriander powder, green chillies and sauté for 2 minutes.
4. Add prawns and fry for 2 minutes.
5. Add the soaked rice and fry for 3 minutes.
6. Add yogurt, garam masala, chilli powder and salt. Mix well.
7. Add 2 cups of water and bring to the boil.
8. Cover the pot and cook on low heat for 20 minutes.
9. Serve hot.

Nutrition information:
Calories: 396 kcal
Protein: 22 g
Fat: 10 g
Carbohydrates: 48 g
Fiber: 2 g

54. Aloo Baingan

Enjoy the delightful flavors of aloo baingan, an Indian dish featuring potatoes and eggplant cooked in a savory curry. This vegan dish is straightforward to prepare and is full of flavor. Serve it over cooked basmati rice to round out the meal.

Serving: Serves 4
Preparation time: 25 minutes
Ready Time: 35 minutes

Ingredients:
- 2 tablespoons olive oil
- 2 cloves garlic, minced
- 2 teaspoons ginger, minced
- 1 tablespoon curry powder
- 1 teaspoon ground cumin
- 2 cups tomato puree
- 1 teaspoon sea salt
- 1 teaspoon sugar
- 2 small eggplants, cut into cubes
- 2 large potatoes, peeled and cubed
- 1/4 cup chopped fresh cilantro

Instructions:
1. Heat the oil in a large skillet over medium-high heat.
2. Add the garlic and ginger, and sauté for 1 minute.
3. Stir in the curry powder and cumin, and cook for 1 minute.
4. Add the tomato puree, salt, and sugar, and bring to a boil.
5. Reduce the heat to low, and add the eggplant and potatoes.
6. Simmer the mixture, stirring occasionally, until the vegetables are cooked through, about 20 minutes.
7. Garnish with the cilantro, and serve hot.

Nutrition information
Calories: 303, Fat: 8g, Saturated Fat: 1g, Carbohydrates: 44g, Fiber: 10g, Protein: 5g, Sodium: 944mg

55. Chicken Saagwala

Chicken Saagwala is an Indian dish that combines the flavors of chicken and spinach cooked in a creamy tomato-based curry. It is a comforting and delicious dish that can be enjoyed either as a main course or side dish.
Serving: 4-6

Preparation Time: 15 minutes
Ready Time: 30 minutes

Ingredients:
-1 lb boneless, skinless chicken thighs
-2 tablespoons vegetable oil
-1 medium onion, chopped
-3 cloves garlic, minced
-1 tablespoon fresh ginger, peeled and grated
-1 teaspoon ground turmeric
-1 teaspoon ground cumin
-1 teaspoon ground coriander
-1 teaspoon garam masala
-Salt and pepper
-2 cups fresh spinach leaves, finely chopped
-1 can diced tomatoes
-1 cup plain yogurt

Instructions:
1. Heat oil in a large skillet over medium heat.
2. Add the onion, garlic, and ginger and sauté for 5 minutes.
3. Add the spices and season with salt and pepper. Cook for 1 minute.
4. Add the chicken and cook for about 8 minutes, stirring occasionally.
5. Add the spinach leaves, diced tomatoes, and yogurt and cook for an additional 10 minutes.
6. Serve over cooked basmati rice.

Nutrition information:
Per Serving:
Calories: 391
Total Fat: 12.7g
Saturated Fat: 4.5g
Cholesterol: 86mg
Sodium: 144mg
Carbohydrate: 28.4g
Fiber: 4.9g
Sugar: 9.5g
Protein: 36.4g

56. Rajma Pulao

Rajma Pulao is a flavorful and protein packed Indian rice dish loaded with kidney beans and spices.
Serving: 4
Preparation Time: 15 minutes
Ready Time: 30-35 minutes

Ingredients:
- 1 cup long grain or basmati rice
- 2 tablespoons oil
- 1 teaspoon cumin seeds
- 1 bay leaf
- 2 cloves
- 1 teaspoon garlic, chopped
- Pinch of asafoetida (hing)
- 1 cup onion, chopped
- 1 teaspoon chilli powder
- 1 teaspoon coriander powder
- 1/2 teaspoon turmeric powder
- 1 cup tomato, chopped
- 1 cup cooked kidney beans (rajma)
- Salt to taste
- 2 cups water

Instructions:
1. Soak the rice in water for at least 30 minutes.
2. Heat oil in a pan and add the cumin seeds, bay leaf, cloves, garlic, and asafoetida.
3. Add the onions and sauté until they are golden brown.
4. Add the chilli powder, coriander powder, and turmeric powder and mix well.
5. Add the tomatoes and cook until they are soft.
6. Add the kidney beans and stir to combine.
7. Add the soaked rice and mix well.
8. Add the water and salt to taste.
9. Bring to a boil, reduce the heat and simmer for 15-20 minutes or until the rice is cooked and the liquid has been absorbed.
10. Serve hot with side dishes of your choice.

Nutrition information (per serving): Calories: 369, Fat: 9g, Sodium: 45mg, Carbohydrates: 61g, Fiber: 6g, Protein: 12g

57. Chicken Pulao

Chicken Pulao is an aromatic, flavorful and colorful dish. It is a one pot dish that is quite easy to make and can be served for lunch or dinner.
Serving: 4
Preparation time: 20 minutes
Ready time: 40 minutes

Ingredients:
2 tablespoons unsalted butter
1 large onion, finely chopped
1 teaspoon freshly grated ginger
2 cloves garlic, minced
1/2 teaspoon ground coriander
1/2 teaspoon garam masala
1 teaspoon ground turmeric
2 whole cardamom pods
1 bay leaf
2 cups long-grain white rice
2 1/2 cups chicken broth
1/2 cup frozen peas
2 boneless, skinless chicken thighs, cut into bite-size pieces
1/4 cup chopped fresh cilantro

Instructions:
1. In a large saucepan, melt the butter over medium heat.
2. Add the onion and cook until softened, about 5 minutes.
3. Add the ginger, garlic, coriander, garam masala, turmeric, cardamom pods and bay leaf, and stir to combine.
4. Add the rice and stir to coat with the spices.
5. Add the chicken broth and bring to a boil.
6. Reduce the heat, cover and simmer until the rice is almost tender, about 15 minutes.
7. Stir in the peas and chicken and cook until the chicken is cooked through and the peas are tender, about 5 minutes.

8. Stir in the cilantro and serve.

Nutrition information:
Calories: 369
Fat: 10 g
Carbohydrates: 42 g
Protein: 20 g
Sodium: 458 mg
Fiber: 3 g

58. Paneer Bhurji

Paneer Bhurji is a popular Indian dish prepared with scrambled paneer (cottage cheese). It is delectable and easy to prepare.
Serving: 6-7
Preparation Time: 15 minutes
Ready Time: 30 minutes

Ingredients:
- 2 cups paneer (cottage cheese), crumbled
- 1 large onion, finely chopped
- 1 medium tomato, finely chopped
- 1 green capsicum, finely chopped
- 1 teaspoon cumin seeds
- 2 green chillies, finely chopped
- 2 tablespoons finely chopped coriander
- 1 teaspoon red chilli powder
- 1 tablespoon garam masala
- 1 tablespoon oil
- Salt to taste

Instructions:
1. Heat oil in a pan and sauté cumin seeds in it.
2. Add chopped onion, tomato, green chillies and capsicum and fry until softened.
3. Add crumbled paneer, red chilli powder, garam masala and salt. Cook for 4-5 minutes and stir continuously.

4. Add coriander and mix well. Cook for a few more minutes until the mixture is dry.
5. Paneer Bhurji is ready, serve hot.

Nutrition information:
Serving Size: 1 (100 g)
Calories: 179 cal
Carbohydrates: 4.6 g
Protein: 12.7 g
Fat: 12.8 g

59. Fish Tikka Masala

Fish Tikka Masala is an Indian dish featuring mild spices and a creamy tomato-based sauce.
Serving: 4
Preparation time: 25 minutes
Ready time: 1 hour

Ingredients:
- 1 pound of boneless fish, cubed
- 2 tablespoons of oil
- 2 onions, chopped
- 2 cloves of garlic, minced
- 1 tablespoon of freshly grated ginger
- 1 teaspoon of ground turmeric
- 1 teaspoon of ground coriander
- 1 teaspoon of garam masala
- 2 tablespoons of tomato paste
- 1 can of diced tomatoes
- 1/2 cup of cream
- 1/2 cup of water
- Salt and pepper to taste

Instructions:
1. Heat oil in a large skillet over medium heat.
2. Add onions and cook until soft, about 5 minutes.

3. Add garlic, ginger, turmeric, coriander, and garam masala and cook for another few minutes, stirring constantly.
4. Add the tomato paste and cook for another minute.
5. Add the diced tomatoes, cream, and water and bring to a simmer.
6. Add the cubed fish and simmer gently for about 20 minutes.
7. Season with salt and pepper to taste.
8. Serve over basmati or jasmine rice.

Nutrition information: One serving of Fish Tikka Masala contains approximately 350 calories, 22 grams of fat, 13 grams of protein, and 19 grams of carbohydrates.

60. Baingan Patiala

Baingan Patiala is a delicious Punjabi dish featuring eggplants smothered in a thick gravy of tomatoes and onions.
Serving: 4
Preparation Time: 10 minutes
Ready Time: 40 minutes

Ingredients:
- 4 eggplants, crushed
- 1 onion, chopped
- 2 tomatoes, chopped
- 2 green chillies, chopped
- 2 tablespoons ghee
- 1 teaspoon cumin
- ½ teaspoon turmeric
- 1 teaspoon coriander powder
- Salt and pepper, to taste
- 2 tablespoons coriander, to garnish

Instructions:
1. Heat the ghee in a heavy-bottomed pan.
2. Add the onions and green chillies and sauté until the onions are golden brown.
3. Add the tomatoes and fry until they are soft and mushy.

4. Add the crushed eggplants, cumin, turmeric, coriander powder and salt and pepper. Stir to combine.
5. Cover and simmer for 25 minutes, or until the eggplants are cooked through.
6. Garnish with coriander and serve hot.

Nutrition information (per serving):
Calories: 191 kcal
Carbohydrates: 12.8 g
Protein: 3.3 g
Fat: 15.5 g
Saturated Fat: 8 g
Cholesterol: 28 mg
Sodium: 434 mg
Potassium: 537 mg
Fiber: 5.3 g

61. Beef Curry

Beef Curry is one of the most popular Southeast Asian dishes that is savory and hearty. It features beef, a variety of spices and herbs, and a flavorful sauce to bring it all together. This classic dish can be made with a few simple Ingredients in less than an hour!
Serving: 4-6
Preparation Time: 15 minutes
Ready Time: 45 minutes

Ingredients:
- 2 lbs beef chuck, cut into 1-inch pieces
- 1 large onion, chopped
- 1 tablespoons peeled and grated fresh ginger
- 2 cloves garlic, minced
- 2 tablespoons curry powder
- 1 teaspoon ground turmeric
- 2 teaspoons ground coriander
- 1 teaspoon ground cumin
- 1 teaspoon chili powder
- 1 13.5-ounce can coconut milk

- 2 tablespoons vegetable or canola oil
- 1 teaspoon sea salt
- ½ teaspoon ground black pepper

Instructions:
1. Heat the oil over medium-high heat in a large skillet.
2. Add the beef to the skillet and sear until browned, about 5 minutes.
3. Add onion, ginger, garlic, curry powder, turmeric, coriander, cumin and chili powder. Cook until the onion is softened, about 5 minutes.
4. Add the coconut milk, salt, and pepper. Bring the mixture to a simmer and reduce the heat to low.
5. Simmer for 30 minutes, stirring occasionally, until the beef is cooked through.
6. Taste and adjust seasoning if desired. Serve over cooked white or brown rice.

Nutrition information (approximate per serving): Calories: 500, Total Fat: 30g, Saturated Fat: 12g, Cholesterol: 70mg, Sodium: 800mg, Carbohydrates: 21g, Fiber: 5g, Sugar: 5g, Protein: 30g.

62. Dal Fry

Dal Fry is a popular Indian dish made by combining yellow lentils (moong dal) cooked with onions, tomatoes, and various spices. It is an incredibly flavorful and nutritious dish that can be enjoyed as the main course.

Serving: 4
Preparation Time: 10 minutes
Ready Time: 30 minutes

Ingredients:
- 1 cup yellow moong dal
- 1/2 teaspoon turmeric powder
- 2 tablespoons oil
- 1 teaspoon cumin seeds
- 2 chopped onions
- 1 chopped tomato
- 2-3 chopped green chilies

- 1/2 teaspoon garam masala
- 2 teaspoons red chili powder
- Salt to taste
- Chopped coriander leaves

Instructions:
1. Wash and soak the yellow moong dal in enough water for 30 minutes.
2. Drain the water and add turmeric powder and enough water to the moong dal so that it is just enough to cook the dal.
3. In a pressure cooker, heat oil and add cumin seeds and onions. Fry until the onions turn golden brown.
4. Add the tomatoes, green chilies, garam masala, red chili powder, and salt. Cook for 3-4 minutes.
5. Add the soaked moong dal and enough water so that the dal is just nice and cook the dal for 2 whistles.
6. Garnish with chopped coriander leaves and serve hot.

Nutrition information: Calories: 207, Total Fat: 7g, Saturated Fat: 1g, Trans Fat: 0g, Cholesterol: 0mg, Sodium: 81mg, Carbohydrates: 29g, Dietary Fiber: 7g, Sugars: 2g, Protein: 9g.

63. Vegetable Khichdi

Vegetable Khichdi is an easy-to-make, one-pot nutritious Indian dish made with rice, lentils, vegetables and spices. It is mild and soothing, very comforting and easy to digest making it an ideal meal for sick or recovering individuals.

Serving: 4
Preparation Time: 10 minutes
Ready Time: 20-25 minutes

Ingredients:
-1/2 cup basmati rice
-1/2 cup toor dal (split pigeon peas)
-1 medium-sized onion, finely chopped
-2 cloves garlic, finely chopped
-1 teaspoon fresh ginger, finely chopped
-1 medium-sized tomato, chopped

- 1/2 cup mixed vegetables (carrots, peas, corn, broccoli, etc.), chopped
- 2 tablespoons clarified butter (ghee) or vegetable oil
- 1 teaspoon cumin seeds
- 1 teaspoon garam masala powder
- 1 teaspoon red chilli powder (optional)
- Salt, to taste

Instructions:
1. Heat the ghee or oil in a deep pan on medium heat.
2. Add the cumin and let it splutter.
3. Add the onion, garlic and ginger and fry till the onions are light brown.
4. Add the vegetables and fry for 4-5 minutes.
5. Add the tomatoes and fry till soft.
6. Add the rice, dal, garam masala powder, red chilli powder (if using) and salt and mix well.
7. Add around 4 cups of water, stir and bring to a boil.
8. Reduce the heat to low, cover the pan and let the khichdi cook for around 15 minutes or until the rice and dal are cooked.
9. Stir and serve hot garnished with a sprig of coriander leaves.

Nutrition information (per serving):
Calories: 349
Fat: 8.6g
Carbohydrates: 52.9g
Protein: 10.8g

64. Chicken Dhansak

Chicken Dhansak is a classic Indian dish made with stewed chicken simmered in a flavorful sauce made with split lentils, spices and herbs. It's a delicious one-pot meal that's hearty, savory and packed with protein and fiber.
Serving: 4 – 6
Preparation Time: 15 minutes
Ready Time: 1 hour

Ingredients:
- 500g boneless, skinless chicken thighs, diced

- 2 medium onions, finely diced
- 2 garlic cloves, finely minced
- 2 tablespoons freshly grated ginger
- 3 tablespoons vegetable oil
- 2 teaspoons ground cumin
- 2 teaspoons ground coriander
- 1 teaspoon ground turmeric
- 2 teaspoons garam masala
- 1/2 teaspoon ground cayenne pepper
- 1 teaspoon salt
- 150g split yellow lentils
- 150g split red lentils
- 500ml chicken stock
- 250ml water
- 1 medium tomato, finely diced
- 2 tablespoons freshly chopped coriander leaves

Instructions:
1. Heat the oil in a large saucepan over a medium-high heat.
2. Add the onions and sauté for 5 minutes until softened.
3. Add the garlic and ginger and sauté for a further 2 minutes.
4. Add the cumin, coriander, turmeric, garam masala, cayenne pepper and salt and cook for 1 minute.
5. Add the chicken and sauté for 5 minutes.
6. Add the lentils and stir to combine.
7. Pour in the chicken stock and water and bring to a boil.
8. Reduce the heat to low, cover and simmer for 30 minutes until the lentils are fully cooked.
9. Finally, stir in the tomato and coriander and simmer for a further 15 minutes.

Nutrition information: Per serving: Calories: 430, Fat: 13g, Carbs: 33g, Protein 35g

65. Matar Paneer

Matar Paneer is a traditional Indian dish made from peas and paneer cooked in spicy tomato gravy. It is a delicious and comforting dish that can be served with either rice or Indian flatbread.

Serving: 4-6
Preparation Time: 15 minutes
Ready Time: 25 minutes

Ingredients:
- 2 tablespoons vegetable oil
- 1/4 teaspoon cumin seed
- 1 small onion, finely chopped
- 1 teaspoon grated ginger
- 2 cloves garlic, minced
- 1/2 teaspoon ground coriander
- 1/4 teaspoon garam masala
- 1/4 teaspoon ground turmeric
- 2 Roma tomatoes, finely chopped
- 1/2 cup frozen peas
- 1/2 cup cubed paneer
- Salt to taste

Instructions:
1. Heat oil in a large skillet over medium heat.
2. Add the cumin seed and onion; cook and stir until the onion is tender, about 5 minutes.
3. Stir in the ginger and garlic; cook for 1 minute.
4. Add the coriander, garam masala and turmeric; cook and stir for 1 minute.
5. Stir in the tomatoes; cook and stir until the tomatoes begin to soften, about 5 minutes.
6. Add the peas and paneer; cook and stir until heated through, about 5 minutes.
7. Season with salt to taste; serve with either rice or Indian flatbread.

Nutrition information: Per serving: Calories 223, Total Fat 11g, Saturated Fat 5g, Sodium 122mg, Total Carbohydrate 18g, Dietary Fiber 5g, Sugars 7g, Protein 8g.

66. Goat Pulao

Goat Pulao is a delicious traditional Pakistani dish full of fragrant spices and herbs with the flavor of tender goat meat.

Serving: 4-6
Preparation Time: 45 minutes
Ready Time: 1 hour

Ingredients:
- 2 tablespoons vegetable oil
- 2 lbs boneless goat, diced
- 1 large onion, diced
- 2 cloves garlic, minced
- 1 tablespoon ginger, minced
- 1 teaspoon cumin
- 1 teaspoon coriander
- 1/2 teaspoon black pepper
- 1/2 teaspoon paprika
- 1 teaspoon red chili powder
- 2 cups uncooked basmati rice
- 4 cups water
- salt to taste

Instructions:
1. Heat oil in a large pot over medium-high heat.
2. Add the goat and cook, stirring occasionally, until it is lightly browned.
3. Add the onion, garlic, and ginger and cook for 5 minutes until fragrant.
4. Add the spices and stir to combine.
5. Add the rice and water and stir to combine.
6. Bring to a boil, reduce heat to low, and cover the pot.
7. Allow the pulao to simmer for 25-30 minutes, or until the rice is fully cooked and the liquid has been absorbed.
8. Season with salt, to taste, and serve.

Nutrition information: Per serving: Calories 398, Fat 5.2g, Saturated fat 0.7g, Carbohydrate 72.2g, Fiber 2.3g, Sugar 3.6g, Protein 12.5g

67. Lauki Chana Dal

Lauki Chana Dal is a nutritious and delicious South Asian dish consisting of cooked bottle gourd and chana dal with a combination of spices.
Serving: 4
Preparation Time: 10 minutes
Ready Time: 25 minutes

Ingredients:
- 2 cups chopped bottle gourd
- 1 cup chana dal
- 1 teaspoon cumin seeds
- 1 teaspoon chopped green chilies
- 1 teaspoon grated ginger
- 1 teaspoon garam masala
- 1 teaspoon coriander powder
- 2 tablespoons oil
- Salt to taste

Instructions:
1. Heat the oil in a pan over medium heat and add the cumin seeds.
2. When the cumin seeds start to sizzle, add the chopped green chilies and grated ginger.
3. When the ginger is fragrant, add the bottle gourd and chana dal.
4. Season with salt and mix well.
5. Cover the pan and cook for 15-20 minutes on low heat, stirring occasionally.
6. Once the dal and gourd are cooked, add the coriander powder and garam masala.
7. Cook for another few minutes and remove from the heat.
8. Serve hot with roti or rice.

Nutrition information:
Calories: 150
Total fat: 5 g
Total carbohydrates: 19 g
Protein: 8 g
Fiber: 7 g
Sodium: 140 mg

68. Shrimp Biryani

Shrimp Biryani is a classic and flavorful Indian rice dish. It's prepared with spices, rice, and shrimp for an unforgettable meal.
Serving: 4
Preparation Time: 15 minutes
Ready Time: 25 minutes

Ingredients:
- 1 pound Medium shrimp (peeled and deveined)
- 1 tablespoon Olive oil
- 1 teaspoon cumin
- 2 cloves garlic (minced)
- 2 teaspoon garam masala
- 1/2 teaspoon ground turmeric
- 1/2 teaspoon cayenne pepper
- 1/2 cup plain yogurt
- 2 cups Basmati rice (soaked in water for at least 30 minutes)
- 2 tablespoons butter
- 1 bay leaf
- 1/2 teaspoon salt
- 2 cups water

Instructions:
1. Heat oil in a large skillet over medium-high heat.
2. Add shrimp and cook for 1-2 minutes until slightly pink.
3. Add cumin, garlic, garam masala, turmeric, and cayenne pepper. Cook for 1 minute.
4. Add yogurt and stir.
5. Add the drained rice, butter, bay leaf, salt, and water. Stir everything together.
6. Bring the mixture to a boil, cover, and reduce to low heat. Cook for 18 minutes.
7. Fluff the rice with a fork before serving.

Nutrition information:
Calories: 200
Fat: 8 g

Carbohydrates: 22 g
Protein: 10 g
Cholesterol: 66 mg
Sodium: 506 mg
Fiber: 1 g

69. Aloo Methi

Aloo Methi is a spicy and delicious Indian dish that is made with potatoes and fresh methi (fenugreek leaves).
Serving: 6
Preparation time: 10 minutes
Ready time: 25 minutes

Ingredients:
- 2 cups of potatoes, cubed
- 1 cup of fresh methi leaves
- 1 teaspoon of cumin seeds
- 1 teaspoon of coriander powder
- ½ teaspoon of turmeric powder
- 2 tablespoons of oil
- Salt to taste

Instructions:
1. Heat oil in a pan over medium heat.
2. Add cumin seeds. Once they start to sizzle, add cubed potatoes and stir-fry for a few minutes.
3. Add salt and all the spices. Mix well and cover the pan. Cook for about 7-8 minutes, stirring occasionally.
4. Add fresh methi leaves and mix well. Cook for another 5-7 minutes, until potatoes are cooked through.
5. Serve hot with chapatis or steamed rice.

Nutrition information: Per serving: 123 kcal, 5.8 g carbohydrates, 4.2 g fats, 7.2 g protein, 0.9 g fiber

70. Lamb Curry

This spicy Lamb Curry is a delicious way to vary up your Greek cuisine. It's great as is or served with sides such as rice, bread, or vegetables.
Serving: Serves 4
Preparation time: 10 minutes
Ready time: 45 minutes

Ingredients:
- 2 tablespoons olive oil
- 2 onions, chopped
- 2 cloves garlic, minced
- 2 pounds lamb, cubed
- 1 teaspoon ground ginger
- 1 teaspoon ground cumin
- 1 teaspoon ground coriander
- 1 teaspoon curry powder
- 1/2 teaspoon salt
- 1/4 teaspoon black pepper
- 1 cinnamon stick
- 2 cups water
- 1 (14.5-ounce) can diced tomatoes
- 1/4 cup fresh cilantro, chopped

Instructions:
1. Heat the olive oil in a large pot over medium heat.
2. Add the onions and garlic and cook for 5 minutes, stirring occasionally.
3. Add the lamb and cook for 5 minutes, stirring occasionally.
4. Add the ginger, cumin, coriander, curry powder, salt, and pepper and stir to combine.
5. Add the cinnamon stick, water, and diced tomatoes. Bring to a boil, reduce the heat to low, and simmer for 30 minutes, stirring occasionally.
6. Remove from the heat and stir in the cilantro. Serve hot.

Nutrition information: Calories per serving: 395; Total Fat: 24.2g; Cholesterol: 83mg; Sodium: 616mg; Total Carbohydrates: 18.3g; Protein: 24.9g; Fiber: 4.7g

71. Kala Chana Curry

Kala Chana Curry is a delicious Indian dish comprising of black chickpeas in a spicy tomato gravy. It is incredibly flavor-packed and a must have for a delicious meal.

Serving: 6-8
Preparation Time: 15 minutes
Ready Time: 45 minutes

Ingredients:
- 1 teaspoon mustard oil
- 750g black chickpeas, soaked and pressure cooked
- 2 onions, chopped
- 3 tomatoes, chopped
- 1 teaspoon cumin powder
- 1 teaspoon coriander powder
- 1 teaspoon turmeric powder
- 1 teaspoon garam masala
- Salt to taste
- 2 tablespoons coriander leaves, chopped

Instructions:
1. Heat mustard oil in a pan over medium heat.
2. Add the onions and sauté until they are lightly browned.
3. Add the tomatoes, cumin powder, coriander powder, turmeric powder, garam masala, and salt. Cook until all the spices are mixed in nicely.
4. Add the cooked black chickpeas to the pan and stir to combine.
5. Simmer the curry for about 20 minutes.
6. Garnish with coriander leaves.
7. Serve Kala Chana Curry over rice or roti.

Nutrition information: (per serving)
Calories: 217 kcal
Fat: 5.2g
Carbohydrates: 33.1g
Protein: 8.6g

72. Chicken Madras

Chicken Madras is an aromatic curry that originates from South India. A traditional dish full of spicy flavors, it's a perfect entree to spice up any dinner menu.
Serving: 4
Preparation Time: 15 minutes
Ready Time: 25 minutes

Ingredients:
- 500g chicken breast, cubed
- 1 large onion, chopped
- 2 cloves garlic, crushed
- 2 tablespoons vegetable oil
- 2 tablespoons Madras curry powder
- 200ml tomato ketchup
- 100ml water
- 1 teaspoon honey
- 1 teaspoon cumin
- Salt and ground black pepper

Instructions:
1. In a large pan, heat the oil on medium heat and add the onion, garlic and chicken.
2. Stir-fry for 3-4 minutes until lightly browned.
3. Add the curry powder, tomato ketchup, water, honey, cumin, salt and pepper.
4. Turn the heat to high and bring to the boil.
5. Reduce the heat to low and simmer for 15-20 minutes, stirring occasionally.
6. Remove from the heat and serve.

Nutrition information: Per serving: 755 calories, 51g fat (9g saturated), 40g carbohydrates, 6g sugar, 67g protein, 6g fiber.

73. Capsicum Masala

Capsicum Masala is a warm, flavorful dish from the northern region of India. This dish is easy to prepare and is a great addition to any Indian meal.

Serving: 8
Preparation Time: 10 minutes
Ready Time: 25 minutes

Ingredients:
- 2 tablespoons of oil
- 1 teaspoon of cumin seeds
- 1 large onion, chopped
- 2 large capsicums, diced
- 2 cloves of garlic, finely chopped
- 2 teaspoons of turmeric
- 2 teaspoons of garam masala
- 2 teaspoons of chilli powder
- 2 cups of diced tomatoes
- 1/2 cup of water
- Salt to taste

Instructions:
1. Heat the oil in a large skillet over medium heat.
2. Add in the cumin seeds and let them sizzle for a few seconds.
3. Add in the onion and sauté until golden.
4. Add in the capsicum and garlic and sauté until softened.
5. Add in the turmeric, garam masala, and chilli powder and mix to combine.
6. Add in the diced tomatoes and water and mix to combine.
7. Reduce the heat to low, cover, and simmer for 15 minutes, stirring occasionally.
8. Taste and adjust the seasoning with salt.
9. Remove from the heat and serve warm.

Nutrition information:
Calories: 170, Total fat: 8g, Cholesterol: 0mg, Sodium: 10mg, Carbohydrates: 20g, Protein: 4g

74. Masoor Khichdi

Masoor Khichdi is a rich and comforting one-pot meal made with red lentils and rice. It is usually seasoned with garam masala and served with dollops of ghee for an added layer of indulgence.

Serving: 4
Preparation Time: 10 minutes
Ready Time: 45 minutes

Ingredients:
- 1 cup masoor dal
- 1 cup basmati rice
- 4 cups water
- 1 teaspoon cumin seeds
- 2 bay leaves
- 1 teaspoon garam masala
- 2 tablespoons clarified butter (ghee)
- 1 onion, finely chopped
- 2 tablespoons chopped green chili (optional)
- 2 tablespoons chopped ginger
- 1 teaspoon turmeric powder
- Salt, to taste

Instructions:
1. Wash and soak the masoor dal and basmati rice for 10 minutes.
2. In a pressure cooker, heat ghee on medium heat. Add the cumin seeds and bay leaves.
3. Now add the chopped onions, green chili, ginger and sauté for 2 minutes.
4. Add in the soaked and drained masoor dal and basmati rice.
5. Add the garam masala, turmeric powder and salt. Stir well.
6. Now pour in the water and pressure cook for 2-3 whistles.
7. Let the pressure release naturally and open the lid.
8. Serve the Masoor Khichdi with dollops of ghee.

Nutrition information:
Calories: 315, Fat: 8g, Sodium: 35mg, Carbohydrates: 50g, Protein: 10g, Fiber: 4g.

75. Fish Fry

Fish Fry is a traditional comfort food dish made with pieces of fish, coated in a light batter, and fried until deliciously crisp.
Serving: 4-5
Preparation Time: 10 minutes
Ready Time: 15 minutes

Ingredients:
- 2 lbs Fish fillets
- 1/4 cup all-purpose flour
- 2 tablespoons dry mustard
- 1 teaspoon salt
- 1/2 teaspoon ground black pepper
- 1 tablespoon garlic powder
- 2 eggs
- 2 tablespoons vegetable oil

Instructions:
1. In a shallow dish, mix together flour, dry mustard, salt, black pepper and garlic powder.
2. Dip each fish fillet into the mixture, making sure to coat every surface.
3. Heat vegetable oil in a large skillet over medium-high heat.
4. In a different bowl, whisk eggs together and then dip the fish fillets in the eggs.
5. Place the fish into the hot oil and fry until golden brown. Flip the fillets over and fry the other side until golden brown.
6. Once done, transfer the fish to a plate lined with paper towels and serve.

Nutrition information:
Calories: 246kcal, Carbohydrates: 6.3g, Protein: 35.8g, Fat: 8.4g, Saturated Fat: 1.6g, Cholesterol: 124mg, Sodium: 487mg, Fiber: 0.7g, Sugar: 0.3g

76. Mushroom Pulao

Mushroom pulao is a delicious, flavorful and easy to make rice dish made with mushrooms, aromatic spices and herbs. This mouthwatering dish can be served as a one-pot meal for any occasion.

Serving: 8
Preparation Time: 10 minutes
Ready Time: 30 minutes

Ingredients:
Rice – 2 cups
Mushrooms – 500 grams
Onion – 1 large (finely chopped)
Ginger garlic paste – 1 teaspoon
Green chillies – 4-5 (slit lengthwise)
Cinnamon – 2 small sticks
Cloves – 6-7
Bay leaves – 2
Cardamom – 4-5
Cumin seeds – 1 teaspoon
Mint leaves – 1 tablespoon (chopped)
Garam masala – 1 teaspoon
Turmeric powder – 1/2 teaspoon
Salt – to taste
Oil – 2 tablespoons

Instructions:
1. Rinse the rice a few times with water and soak for 15 minutes.
2. Heat oil in a pressure cooker. Add cumin seeds, cinnamon, cloves, bay leaves and cardamom and sauté for a few seconds.
3. Add the chopped onions and sauté until golden brown.
4. Add the ginger garlic paste and green chillies and sauté for a minute.
5. Add the mushrooms and sauté for 8-10 minutes.
6. Add the mint leaves, turmeric powder, garam masala and salt and sauté for a minute.
7. Add the soaked rice and mix well.
8. Add 2 cups of water, close the lid of the cooker and pressure cook for 3-4 whistles.
9. Turn off the heat and let the steam escape before opening the lid.
10. Fluff the rice gently with a fork and serve hot with a dollop of ghee or pickle.

Nutrition information:
Calories – 120 kcal
Fat – 4 g
Protein – 6 g
Carbohydrates – 17 g
Fiber – 1 g

77. Chicken Handi

Chicken Handi is a delicious dish, orignally from India, prepared with chicken, tomatoes, spices and a base of yogurt or cream.
Serving: 4
Preparation time: 10 minutes
Ready time: 30 minutes

Ingredients:
1 lb of boneless chicken, 2 tablespoons of plain yogurt, 1 teaspoon of coriander powder, 1 teaspoon of cumin powder, 1 onion minced, 2 tomatoes pureed, 5 cloves of garlic minced, 2 jalapeños chopped, 2 tablespoons of vegetable oil, 2 tablespoons of lemon juice, a pinch of garam masala, 2 tablespoons of cilantro chopped.

Instructions:
1. Heat the oil in a skillet or saucepan on medium heat.
2. Add the garlic, onions, jalapeño, coriander and cumin to the pan and cook for 3 minutes.
3. Add the chicken and cook for 5 minutes until the chicken is cooked through.
4. Add the tomato puree and cook for 2 minutes.
5. Add the yogurt, salt and lemon juice.
6. Reduce heat to low and cook for 15 minutes, stirring occasionally.
7. Add a pinch of garam masala and chopped cilantro and stir to combine.
8. Serve the chicken handi with cooked rice.

Nutrition information: Calories: 309, Fat: 17 g, Protein: 28 g, Carbohydrates: 11 g, Fiber: 2 g, Cholesterol: 72 mg, Sodium: 143 mg.

78. Palak Corn

Palak Corn is an Indian dish prepared with a combination of spinach and sweetcorn. This delectable dish is a perfect side for all your festive meals or special occasions.
Serving: 4-5
Preparation Time: 15 minutes
Ready Time: 30 minutes

Ingredients:
- 2 cups frozen sweetcorn
- 2-3 cups of chopped spinach
- 1/4 teaspoon of cumin powder
- 1/4 teaspoon of garam masala
- 2 tablespoons of oil
- Salt to taste

Instructions:
1. Heat oil in a pan, add cumin powder and garam masala.
2. Add the frozen sweetcorn to the pan and sauté over medium flame for 5 minutes.
3. Add the chopped spinach and salt. Mix and cook for another 7-8 minutes or until soft.
4. Serve hot as a side with your meal of choice.

Nutrition information:
Calories: 125 kcal, Carbohydrates: 16.4 g, Protein: 4.2 g, Fat: 6.5 g, Cholesterol: 0.0 mg, Sodium: 375.9 mg, Fiber: 3.2 g, Sugar: 4.3 g.

79. Baingan Bhurta

Baingan Bhurta is a flavorful side dish made with mashed roasted eggplant that is mixed with onions and spices. This dish is a popular North Indian side dish popularly served with chapati or naan.
Serving: 4
Preparation Time: 10 minutes

Ready Time: 25 minutes

Ingredients:
- 1 large eggplant
- 1 medium onion, chopped
- 3 green chilies, chopped
- 1 teaspoon cumin powder
- ½ teaspoon coriander powder
- ¼ teaspoon turmeric powder
- 2 tablespoons oil
- Salt to taste

Instructions:
1. Preheat oven to 400°F/200°C.
2. Place the eggplant on a baking tray and bake for about 25 minutes until the eggplant is tender and cooked through.
3. Once the eggplant is done, remove from the oven and let it cool.
4. When the eggplant is cool enough to handle, peel off the skin and mash the flesh with a spoon or a fork.
5. Heat oil in a large pan over medium-high heat.
6. Once hot, add chopped onion and green chilies. Saute for a few minutes until the onion becomes soft and translucent.
7. Add cumin powder, coriander powder, turmeric powder, and salt. Mix everything well and cook for another minute.
8. Add the mashed eggplant and mix everything together. Cook for about 5 minutes, stirring occasionally.
9. Serve hot with chapati or naan.

Nutrition information:
Calories: 111
Fat: 6.4 g
Carbs: 12.4 g
Protein: 2.3 g
Fiber: 3.7 g

80. Keema Pulao

Keema pulao is a flavorful and fragrant traditional Indian dish, and is especially popular in the northern part of the country. It's a pulao (or pilaf) made with cooked minced meat (keema) such as lamb, and fragrant Basmati rice.

Serving: 4
Preparation time: 15 mins
Ready time: 50 mins

Ingredients:
- 2 cups Basmati Rice
- 1 lb lean minced meat such as lamb, beef or chicken
- 2 Onions, chopped
- 2 Tomatoes, chopped
- 1 teaspoon Ginger-Garlic paste
- 2 Green chilies, chopped
- 1 teaspoon Red chili powder
- 1 teaspoon Coriander powder
- 1 teaspoon Cumin powder
- Juice of 1 Lemon
- 2 tablespoons Ghee
- 2 tablespoons Vegetable oil
- A handful of finely chopped Coriander leaves
- 2 Cardamom pods
- 2 Cloves
- 1 teaspoon Cumin seeds
- 2 Bay leaves
- Salt to taste

Instructions:
1. Wash and soak the Basmati Rice in cold water for 30 mins.
2. Heat the ghee and oil in a deep pan.
3. Add the cumin seeds, cardamom pods and cloves.
4. When it begins to splutter, add the bay leaves, onion, ginger-garlic paste, green chilies and fry until the onions are golden brown.
5. Add the minced meat and sauté until it changes color.
6. Add the chopped tomatoes, red chili powder, coriander powder and cumin powder. Sauté for a few minutes until the tomatoes are mushy.
7. Add the soaked Basmati Rice and mix it with the spice mixture.
8. Add 2 cups of water to the rice and bring it to a boil.

9. Simmer the heat and cook until the rice is fully cooked and the water has been absorbed.
10. Add the lemon juice and mix it gently.
11. Garnish the Keema Pulao with the coriander leaves and serve hot.

Nutrition information: per serving: 441 calories, 28 gram protein, 33 gram fat, 18 gram carbohydrates

81. Rajma Chawal

Rajma Chawal is a timeless classic from North India, packed full of flavour and nourishment. It is made with red kidney beans (known as rajma) and rice cooked together in a fragrant tomato-based sauce.
Serving: 4-6
Preparation time: 15 minutes
Ready time: 45 minutes

Ingredients:
-2 cups red kidney beans (rajma), soaked overnight and drained
-2 tablespoons vegetable oil
-1 large onion, chopped
-2 teaspoons ginger garlic paste
-2 large tomatoes, chopped
-3 teaspoons garam masala
-1 teaspoon red chilli powder
-Salt, to taste
-2 cups basmati rice, washed and drained

Instructions:
1. Heat the oil in a large pot over medium-high heat.
2. Add the onions and sauté for 3-4 minutes until slightly softened.
3. Add the ginger garlic paste and sauté for another minute.
4. Add the chopped tomatoes and stir for 3-4 minutes until softened.
5. Add the garam masala, red chilli powder, and salt to taste and stir.
6. Add the drained kidney beans and stir to combine.
7. Add 3 cups of hot water and bring to boil.
8. Simmer for 10-15 minutes until the beans are cooked through.
9. Add the basmati rice to the pot and mix to combine.

10. Lower the heat to medium-low and simmer gently for 20-25 minutes until the rice is cooked and the liquid has been absorbed.
11. Fluff the rice with a fork before serving.

Nutrition information (per serving):
Calories: 467 kcal
Fat: 11 g
Carbohydrates: 73 g
Protein: 16 g
Fiber: 12 g

82. Chicken Sukka

Chicken Sukka is a flavorful dry curry dish of South Indian cuisine. It is made with chicken and a special blend of spices.
Serving: Serves 4
Preparation Time: 10 minutes
Ready Time: 25 minutes

Ingredients:
-1 cup oil
-3 onions, finely chopped
-1/2 tsp mustard seeds
-1 1/2 tbsp ginger garlic paste
-8-10 curry leaves
-Salt to taste
-2 tsp chili powder
-1 tsp garam masala
-2 cups of chicken, chopped
-1/2 cup shredded coconut
-1/4 cup chopped coriander leaves

Instructions:
1. Heat oil in a pan over medium-high heat.
2. Add onions and fry until golden brown.
3. Add mustard seeds, ginger garlic paste, curry leaves, and salt.
4. Mix in chili powder and garam masala and stir for 1 minute.
5. Add chicken and fry for 5-7 minutes.

6. Add shredded coconut, mix and cook for 3 minutes.
7. Lastly, add coriander leaves and mix well.
8. Serve with steamed rice.

Nutrition information: Calories: 467, Protein: 17 g, Fat: 35 g, Carbohydrates: 16 g, Sodium: 359 mg, Fiber: 3 g

83. Paneer Jalfrezi

Paneer Jalfrezi is a tasty and spicy dish that packs an incredible flavor punch. It's made with generous chunks of paneer in a spicy tomato-based sauce that's flavored with traditional Indian spices.
Serving: 4
Preparation time: 10 minutes
Ready time: 20 minutes

Ingredients:
- 400g paneer, cubed
- 2 medium onions, finely chopped
- 4 cloves of garlic, crushed
- 2 green chillies, chopped
- 1 tomato, chopped
- 1 teaspoon cumin powder
- 1 teaspoon coriander powder
- 1 teaspoon garam masala
- 2 tablespoons oil
- Salt to taste

Instructions:
1. Heat the oil in a pan over medium heat.
2. Add the onions and garlic and cook until the onions are softened.
3. Add the green chillies, tomato, cumin powder, coriander powder and garam masala and cook for a few minutes.
4. Add the paneer cubes and cook for a few minutes until it is cooked through.
5. Add salt to taste and cook for a few more minutes.
6. Serve hot with chapatti, naan or rice.

Nutrition information: per serving:
Calories: 410
Protein: 15.9g
Carbs: 6.9g
Fat: 34.3g

84. Prawn Masala

Prawn Masala is an Indian dish consisting of marinated prawns cooked in a masala sauce. It is a popular dish in South India and goes well with basmati rice, naan, roti, or parathas.
Serving: 4
Preparation time: 10 minutes
Ready time: 25 minutes

Ingredients:
- 1 pound of jumbo prawns
- 2 tablespoons of curry powder
- 1 tablespoon of garam masala powder
- 2 tablespoons of freshly grated ginger
- 2 cloves of garlic, finely minced
- 2 tablespoons of vegetable oil
- 2 tablespoons of tomato paste
- 1/3 cup of unsalted cashew nuts
- 1 teaspoon of dried fenugreek leaves
- Salt to taste

Instructions:
1. Rinse and pat dry the prawns and set aside.
2. In a bowl, combine the curry powder and garam masala. Add in the ginger, garlic and enough oil to create a paste.
3. Place the marinated prawns in a heated pan, stirring until they are lightly browned.
4. Add in the tomato paste, cashew nuts, fenugreek leaves, and the masala paste. Cook for another 2 minutes, stirring constantly.
5. Reduce the heat to low and simmer for about 15 minutes.
6. Serve hot with basmati rice, naan, roti, or parathas.

Nutrition information: per serving: Calories: 181, Fat: 9g, Carbohydrates: 5.2g, Protein: 14g

85. Aloo Dum

Aloo Dum is a delicious Indian-style dish made with potatoes cooked in a spicy tomato based gravy. It takes less than an hour to make and is a classic family favorite.
Serving: Serves 4
Preparation Time: 10 minutes
Ready Time: 50 minutes

Ingredients:
- 4 potatoes, peeled and cut into cubes
- 2 teaspoons cumin seeds
- 1 teaspoon garam masala
- 1 teaspoon chili powder
- 2 bay leaves
- 1 teaspoon turmeric powder
- 2 tablespoons oil
- 1/4 cup water
- 1 onion, diced
- 2 tomatoes, diced
- 2 cloves garlic, minced
- 1 tablespoon ginger, grated
- 1 teaspoon sugar

Instructions:
1. Heat oil in a large pan over medium heat.
2. Add cumin seeds, bay leaves, and garam masala and stir until they become fragrant, about 1 minute.
3. Add potatoes, chili powder, and turmeric powder and stir until the spices coat the potatoes.
4. Cover and cook for about 5 minutes or until potatoes are tender.
5. Add the onion, tomatoes, garlic, ginger, and sugar and stir.
6. Cover and cook for another 5 minutes or until the tomatoes and onion are cooked.
7. Add 1/4 cup of water and stir.

8. Cover and cook for another 10 minutes or until the sauce has thickened.
9. Serve hot.

Nutrition information:
Calories – 99 kcal, Carbohydrates – 15 g, Protein – 3 g, Fat – 4 g, Sodium – 0 mg, Sugar – 4 g.

86. Lamb Biryani

Lamb Biryani is a royal Indian dish made with basmati rice, aromatic spices, and tender lamb. This flavorful dish is sure to be a hit at any gathering.
Serving: Serves 6-8
Preparation Time: 15 minutes
Ready Time: 1 hour

Ingredients:
- 2 lbs lamb, cut into 1" cubes
- 2 cups basmati rice, washed and soaked for 20 minutes
- 2 tablespoons ghee
- 2 onions, finely chopped
- 2 cloves garlic, minced
- 2 tablespoons ginger, grated
- 2 teaspoons ground cumin
- 2 teaspoons ground coriander
- 1 teaspoon ground turmeric
- 4 cardamom pods
- 1 teaspoon ground cinnamon
-1 teaspoon red chili powder
- 4 tomatoes, chopped
- 2 tablespoons plain yogurt
- 1 tablespoon chopped fresh cilantro plus more for garnish
- 2 cups water

Instructions:
1. Heat the ghee in a large pot over medium heat.

2. Add the onions, garlic, ginger, and spices and cook until the onions are softened, about 5 minutes.
3. Add the tomatoes and cook for an additional 3 minutes.
4. Add the lamb and cook until the lamb is browned, about 10 minutes.
5. Add the yogurt, cilantro and water. Stir and bring to a boil.
6. Add the rice, stir, reduce heat to low and cover. Simmer for 20 minutes.
7. Uncover and stir gently with a fork. Cover and simmer for an additional 10 minutes.
8. Serve with extra cilantro for garnish.

Nutrition information:
Calories: 559 kcal, Carbohydrates: 60.6 g, Protein: 29.3 g, Fat: 21.2 g, Saturated Fat: 7.7 g, Cholesterol: 109 mg, Sodium: 117 mg, Potassium: 512 mg, Fiber: 3.2 g, Sugar: 6.2 g, Vitamin A: 254 IU, Vitamin C: 19 mg, Calcium: 74 mg, Iron: 5 mg.

87. Vegetable Sambar

Vegetable Sambar is a traditional South Indian dish that is made with a blend of vegetables cooked in a flavorful and spicy tamarind broth.
Serving: 4
Preparation Time: 15 minutes
Ready Time: 45 minutes

Ingredients:
- 2 tablespoons tamarind paste
- 2 potatoes, peeled and diced
- 1 medium onion, chopped
- 2 carrots, diced
- 1/2 cup green beans, chopped
- 1/2 cup frozen peas
- 1/2 cup diced tomatoes
- 1 teaspoon ground turmeric
- 3 tablespoons sambar powder
- 1/2 teaspoon mustard seeds
- Salt, to taste

Instructions:
1. In a large pot, add the tamarind paste, potatoes, onion, carrots, green beans, peas, tomatoes, turmeric, sambar powder, and mustard seeds.
2. Bring the mixture to a boil over medium-high heat, then reduce the heat to low and simmer for 20 minutes, stirring occasionally.
3. Add salt to taste and simmer for 10 more minutes, or until the vegetables are tender.
4. Serve the sambar hot with cooked rice.

Nutrition information: Per serving, Vegetable Sambar contains approximately 305 calories, 7g fat, 56g carbohydrates, and 8g protein.

88. Chicken Chettinad

This traditional Indian dish called Chicken Chettinad is a flavorful South Indian chicken curry. It is a rich and spicy curry with the unique flavor of freshly ground spices.
Serving: This dish serves 4 people.
Preparation time: Approximately 10 minutes.
Ready time: Approximately 40 minutes.

Ingredients:
- 2 tablespoons of vegetable oil
- 2 onions, diced
- 6 cloves garlic, minced
- 2 tablespoons of grated ginger
- 1 teaspoon of turmeric powder
- 3 tablespoons of coriander powder
- 1 teaspoon of cumin powder
- 1 teaspoon of black pepper powder
- 2 tablespoons of chaat masala
- 2 tablespoons of chile-garlic paste
- 2 pounds of chicken (breast or thighs), cut into cubes
- 2 tomatoes, diced
- 1 cup of coconut milk
- Salt, to taste

Instructions:
1. Heat the oil in a large pot over medium-high heat.
2. Add the onions, garlic and ginger and cook until translucent, about 5 minutes.
3. Add the turmeric, coriander, cumin and black pepper. Stir for 2 minutes.
4. Add the chaat masala and chile-garlic paste and stir for 1 minute.
5. Add the chicken and tomatoes and stir for 5 minutes.
6. Pour the coconut milk and stir to combine. Bring the mixture to a boil, reduce heat and simmer for 15 minutes.
7. Taste and add salt to taste.
8. Cook for an additional 10 minutes on low heat.

Nutrition information: Each serving provides approximately 310 calories, 17.3g fat, 1.9g saturated fat, 40.2g protein, 6.9g carbohydrates and 2.8g fibre.

89. Methi Matar Malai

Methi Matar Malai is a popular north Indian dish featuring flavorful fenugreek leaves and green peas in a creamy gravy.
Serving: 4
Preparation time: 10 minutes
Ready time: 45 minutes

Ingredients:
- 1 cup green peas
- 2 cups chopped fresh fenugreek leaves (methi)
- 2-3 green chillies, chopped
- 2 tablespoons cashew paste
- 2 tablespoons tomato paste
- 2 tablespoons fresh ginger-garlic paste
- 1 teaspoon garam masala
- 1 teaspoon cumin powder
- 1 teaspoon coriander powder
- 2 tablespoons dried fenugreek leaves (kasuri methi)
- 2 tablespoons cream
- 3 tablespoons oil

- Salt to taste

Instructions:
1. Heat oil in a pan and add the ginger-garlic paste and fry for a minute.
2. Add in the chopped fenugreek leaves and green chillies and fry until the leaves turn soft.
3. Add the cashew paste and tomato paste and fry for a few minutes.
4. Add the green peas and sauté for a few minutes.
5. Now add the garam masala, cumin powder and coriander powder and mix well.
6. Add the dried fenugreek leaves and cream and mix well.
7. Add water as needed and cook on low flame for 25-30 minutes, until the peas are cooked and the gravy thickens.
8. Garnish with fresh cream and serve hot.

Nutrition information:
Calories: 146 kcal, Carbohydrates: 12.3g, Protein: 4.3g, Fat: 9.4g, Sodium: 302mg, Sugar: 3.0g

90. Mushroom Rice

Mushroom Rice is a simple yet flavourful dish that is perfect for a light meal or as a side dish for a bigger meal. Bursting with savory mushrooms and chewy rice, this dish brings out the best of both!
Serving - 4
Preparation time - 10 minutes
Ready time - 25 minutes

Ingredients:
- 2 tablespoons of vegetable oil
- 2 tablespoons of fresh garlic, minced
- 8 ounces of sliced mushrooms
- Dash of salt and pepper
- 2 cups of long-grain white rice
- 3¾ cups of vegetable broth

Instructions:
1. Heat the oil in a large skillet over medium-high heat.

2. Add the garlic and mushrooms and season with a dash of salt and pepper. Cook, stirring occasionally, until the mushrooms are softened, about 5 minutes.
3. Add the rice and stir until lightly toasted, about 2 minutes.
4. Add the vegetable broth and bring to a boil. Reduce the heat to low and cover. Simmer until the rice is cooked through, about 15 minutes.
5. Serve and enjoy!

Nutrition information -
- Calories: 232 kcal
- Protein: 4 g
- Fat: 7.5 g
- Sodium: 570 mg
- Carbohydrates: 35 g
- Fiber: 1.5 g

91. Mutton Biryani

Mutton Biryani is an Indian specialty dish made with fragrant basmati rice, spices, and succulent pieces of mutton. It is an indulgent and delicious main course that is sure to please.
Serving: 6-8 servings
Preparation Time: 30 minutes
Ready Time: 2-3 hours

Ingredients:
- 2lbs mutton
- 2 cups Basmati rice
- 2 onions, chopped
- 2-3 tomatoes, chopped
- 1 ½ cup plain yogurt
- 2 tablespoons ginger garlic paste
- 2-3 green chillies, chopped
- 1 teaspoon coriander powder
- 1 teaspoon garam masala
- 2 bay leaves
- 2-3 cardamom pods
- 2-3 cinnamon sticks

- 5-6 cloves
- Salt, to taste
- 2 tablespoons ghee
- ½ cup fried onions, thinly sliced
- 2-3 green chillies, slit
- 2 tablespoons coriander leaves, chopped

Instructions:
1. Wash the mutton and marinate it with yogurt, ginger garlic paste, green chillies, coriander powder, garam masala, and salt.
2. Keep aside for 2-3 hours.
3. Heat ghee in a pan and add bay leaves, cardamom, cloves and cinnamon.
4. Add marinated mutton and fry.
5. When it is almost done, add tomatoes and onions and fry for 5-7 minutes.
6. Add basmati rice and fry for 2-3 minutes.
7. Add 3 cups of boiling water and simmer for 10-15 minutes.
8. Add fried onions and chopped coriander leaves.
9. Cook until the rice is done and all the water is absorbed.
10. Serve hot with raita (Indian yogurt dip).

Nutrition information: per serving: 193 calories, 8 g fat, 21 g protein, 15 g carbohydrates, 1 g fiber.

92. Chole Pulao

Chole pulao is a classic North Indian dish, consisting of spicy chickpeas, fragrant spices, and long grained Basmati rice. It is wonderfully flavorful and satisfying, and perfect for any occasion.
Serving: 6
Preparation time: 20 minutes
Ready time: 40 minutes

Ingredients:
- 2 cups long grained Basmati rice
- 2 cups cooked chickpeas
- 2 tablespoons olive oil

- 2 cloves garlic, finely chopped
- 1 onion, finely chopped
- 2 teaspoons ground cumin
- 2 teaspoons ground coriander
- 1 teaspoon ground turmeric
- 2 canned tomatoes, chopped
- 1 teaspoon chili powder
- 1 cup vegetable stock
- Salt to taste

Instructions:
1. Rinse the Basmati rice in cold water until it is clean.
2. Heat the oil in a large saucepan over low heat. Add the garlic and onion and sauté until the onion is softened.
3. Add the cumin, coriander, and turmeric and cook for 2 minutes.
4. Add the tomatoes and chili powder and cook for a few minutes, stirring occasionally.
5. Add the vegetable stock and the cooked chickpeas. Bring to a boil.
6. Add the Basmati rice and stir until everything is combined.
7. Cover the pan with a lid and reduce the heat to low. Simmer for 18-20 minutes.
8. Remove from heat and let it rest for 5 minutes before serving.

Nutrition information:
Calories: 315 kcal
Carbohydrates: 44.8 g
Protein: 7.5 g
Fat: 11.0 g
Fiber: 7.5 g

93. Egg Fried Rice

Egg Fried Rice is a popular Chinese dish that is enjoyed all around the world. This delicious dish is simple and quick to make, and packed with amazing flavor.
Serving: 4
Preparation time: 10 minutes
Ready time: 20 minutes

Ingredients:
- 3 cups cooked rice
- 2 eggs
- 2 tablespoons vegetable oil
- 2 tablespoons soy sauce
- 2 cloves garlic, minced
- 1/4 cup chopped green onion
- 1/4 cup frozen peas, thawed

Instructions:
1. Heat vegetable oil in a large skillet over medium heat.
2. Crack eggs into the skillet, stirring until cooked through.
3. Add garlic and green onion and sauté for 1 minute.
4. Add cooked rice, and stir-fry for 5 minutes.
5. Add peas and soy sauce, stir-fry for another 5 minutes.
6. Serve hot.

Nutrition information: Per serving, Egg Fried Rice contains 325 calories, 10.5g fat, 45g carbohydrates, and 8.5g protein.

94. Aloo Gajar

Aloo Gajar is an aromatic North Indian dish made with potatoes, carrots, and spices. The carrots and potatoes give this dish a nutritious boost with flavor and texture. It is a simple and delicious side dish often served with roti or rice.

Serving: 4
Preparation time: 15 minutes
Ready time: 25 minutes

Ingredients:
- 2 tablespoons vegetable oil
- 1 teaspoon cumin seeds
- 1 large onion, finely chopped
- 2 cloves garlic, minced
- 1 teaspoon ground ginger
- ½ teaspoon ground cumin

- ½ teaspoon garam masala
- 2 large potatoes, cubed
- 2 medium carrots, chopped
- 1 teaspoon turmeric
- ¼ teaspoon red chili powder
- 2 tablespoons water
- 2 tablespoons fresh coriander leaves, chopped
- Salt to taste

Instructions:
1. Heat the oil in a large pan over medium-high heat.
2. Add the cumin seeds and cook until they start to crackle, about 30 seconds.
3. Add the onion and garlic and cook until the onion is lightly golden, about 3 minutes.
4. Stir in the ginger, cumin, and garam masala and cook for 1 minute.
5. Add the potatoes, carrots, turmeric, and red chili powder. Cook for 3 minutes, stirring frequently.
6. Add the water to the pan and bring to a simmer.
7. Cover the pan and simmer until the vegetables are tender, about 10 minutes.
8. Garnish with the fresh coriander leaves and salt to taste.

Nutrition information: Per serving, this dish provides 166 calories, 6.2g fat, 27mg sodium, 495 mg potassium, 14.9g carbohydrates, 2g fiber, and 2.9g protein.

95. Masoor Curry

Masoor curry is a flavorful, quick and easy lentil curry with tomatoes and warm spices. It has the perfect balance of tart-sweet-tangy flavor and is great when served with roti, paratha, or plain rice.
Serving: 4
Preparation Time: 10 mins
Ready Time: 15 mins

Ingredients:
- 2 tablespoons of vegetable oil

- 2 cloves of garlic, minced
- 1 teaspoon of ginger, grated
- 1 onion, diced
- 1 teaspoon of cumin
- 1 teaspoon of coriander
- 1 teaspoon of garam masala
- ½ teaspoon of chili powder
- 1 cup of split red masoor lentils
- 1 can (14.5 ounces) of diced tomatoes
- 2 cups of water
- Salt and pepper to taste

Instructions:
1. Heat the oil in a large saucepan over medium heat.
2. Add the garlic, ginger, and onion and sauté for 2 minutes.
3. Add the cumin, coriander, garam masala, and chili powder and sauté for another minute.
4. Add the lentils, tomatoes, and water and stir to combine.
5. Bring to a boil, reduce heat and simmer until the lentils are tender, about 10 minutes.
6. Season with salt and pepper to taste.
7. Serve with roti, paratha, or plain rice.

Nutrition information: Calories: 311kcal, Carbohydrates: 42g, Protein: 13g, Fat: 10g, Cholesterol: 0mg, Sodium: 109mg, Fiber: 11g, Sugar: 5g, Vitamin A: 345IU, Vitamin C: 12.2mg, Calcium: 70mg, Iron: 3.6mg.

96. Vegetable Curry

Vegetable Curry is an easy delicious meal that can be enjoyed as a side or main dish. It is made with fresh vegetables and a light curry sauce, making it the perfect comforting meal.
Serving: 4
Preparation Time: 15 minutes
Ready Time: 25 minutes

Ingredients:

- 1/2 red onion, diced
- 1 red pepper, diced
- 1 green pepper, diced
- 1 head of cauliflower, cut into florets
- 1/2 cup frozen peas
- 2 cloves garlic, minced
- 2 tablespoons olive oil
- 2 tablespoons curry powder
- 1 teaspoon turmeric
- 1/2 teaspoon cumin
- 1 (14 oz) can coconut milk

Instructions:
1. In a large saucepan, heat olive oil over medium heat.
2. Add in the onion and red and green peppers and cook for 5 minutes.
3. Add the garlic and cook for an additional 1 minute.
4. Add the cauliflower, peas, curry powder, turmeric and cumin. Stir to combine and cook for 3 minutes.
5. Pour in the coconut milk and stir to combine. Bring to a simmer and cook for 10 minutes.
6. Serve with your favorite sides and enjoy.

Nutrition information:
calories: 190, fat: 13g, saturated fat: 10g, carbohydrates: 13g, fiber: 4g, sugar: 5g, protein: 4g

97. Chicken Kadai

Chicken Kadai is a delicious, Indian style chicken curry made with fresh herbs and spices. It is a hearty meal with a rich sauce and can be enjoyed with flatbread, basmati rice or pulao.
Serving: 4
Preparation Time: 15 minutes
Ready :Time 40 minutes

Ingredients:
- 500 gms boneless chicken, cut into cubes
- 4 tsp kersi masala

- 2 medium sized onions, finely chopped
- 2 tomatoes, chopped
- 2-3 green chillies, chopped
- 1 tbsp of ginger and garlic paste
- 2-3 teaspoon of coriander powder
- 2 teaspoon of red chilli powder
- 1/2 teaspoon of garam masala
- 2-3 teaspoon of cumin seeds
- 2 tablespoon of ghee
- 1 tablespoon of freshly chopped coriander leaves
- Salt to taste

Instructions:
1. Heat ghee in a pan. Add cumin seeds and fry for a few seconds.
2. Add onions and fry till golden brown.
3. Add ginger and garlic paste and fry for a few minutes.
4. Add tomato and all the spices and fry until the oil separates from the masala.
5. Add chicken cubes and fry for 5-7 minutes on medium heat.
6. Add 1 cup of water and cook for 15-20 minutes till the chicken is tender.
7. Garnish with freshly chopped coriander leaves and serve with roti or rice.

Nutrition information:
Calories: 343 kcal, Carbohydrates: 16 g, Protein: 30 g, Fat: 18 g, Saturated Fat: 5 g, Cholesterol: 90 mg, Sodium: 192 mg, Potassium: 851 mg, Fiber: 5 g, Sugar: 6 g, Vitamin A: 887 IU, Vitamin C: 48 mg, Calcium: 63 mg, Iron: 2 mg

98. Paneer Tikki Masala

Paneer Tikki Masala is a popular Pakistani dish made with paneer (Indian cottage cheese), tomatoes, and other spices. This dish is often served with roti (flatbread) or naan and a side of salad or mint chutney.
Serving: 4
Preparation time: 15 minutes
Ready time: 25 minutes

Ingredients:
- 400g Paneer, diced
- 2 Onions, diced
- 2 Tomatoes, chopped
- 2 Green Chillies, chopped
- 2 tsp Ginger-Garlic Paste
- 1 tsp Cumin Powder
- 2 tsp Coriander Powder
- 2 tsp Garam Masala
- 1 tsp Red Chilli Powder
- 2 tbsp Oil
- Salt to taste
- Chopped Coriander Leaves, to garnish

Instructions:
1. Heat oil in a pan over medium heat.
2. Add the onions and fry until they are golden brown.
3. Add the ginger-garlic paste, cumin powder, coriander powder, garam masala and red chilli powder and fry for a few minutes.
4. Add the tomatoes and fry until they are cooked through.
5. Add the paneer and fry for a few minutes.
6. Add 2-3 tablespoons of water and stir to combine.
7. Simmer until the paneer is cooked through.
8. Garnish with chopped coriander leaves and serve with roti or naan.

Nutrition information:
- Calories: 400
- Total Fat: 17 g
- Saturated Fat: 7 g
- Cholesterol: 19 mg
- Sodium: 134 mg
- Total Carbohydrates: 26 g
- Dietary Fiber: 4 g
- Sugars: 8 g
- Protein: 16 g

CONCLUSION

Pressure Cooker Curry Magic: 98 Quick and Flavorful Recipes for Authentic Curries is a great cookbook for new and experienced cooks alike, allowing the user to create delicious curries quickly and easily. This cookbook provides an array of recipes that make use of a readily available and affordable pressure cooker to speed up cookingprocesses and ensure an appetizing final result. With easy-to-follow instructions and a selection of flavorful spices and ingredients, this cookbook is sure to show even novice cooks how to make restaurant-style curries at home.

The 98 recipes offered by Pressure Cooker Curry Magic are varied and are sure to include something to suit everyone's taste buds. From traditional North Indian and South Indian curries to more creative fusion dishes, the recipes provide a range of flavors and styles that make curries even more exciting. For those who are short on time but still want to include curries in their weekly meal plan, the pressure cooker recipes are a great way to make delicious dishes without sacrificing flavor.

The recipes employed throughout Pressure Cooker Curry Magic are simple, yet result in bold and flavorful dishes. The pressure cooker is a great tool that locks in flavor while also reducing the cooking time for the dishes. This cookbook contains recipes that accommodate a range of dietary preferences, including gluten-free, vegan, and vegetarian options. Additionally, for those who like to experiment, there is also the option to adjust the ingredients and spices to add new flavors to the dishes.

All in all, Pressure Cooker Curry Magic provides a modern spin on traditional curry recipes. With quick and easy recipes made possible by the pressure cooker, this cookbook is a great resource for creating flavorful and satisfying curries with minimal effort. The recipes included are varied and allow for experimentation and adjustments that are sure to yield some delicious results. Whether for an experienced cook or a novice who is just starting out, Pressure Cooker Curry Magic is an invaluable resource for cooking up some delicious authentic curries with ease.

Printed in Great Britain
by Amazon